Naked Tuesday

Naked Tuesday

THE KIDS ARE GONE, THE HOUSE
IS EMPTY, TUESDAY IS MY DAY

• • •

Judy Kucharuk

ISBN-13: 9781533481313
ISBN-10: 1533481318
Library of Congress Control Number: 2016909292
CreateSpace Independent Publishing Platform
North Charleston, South Carolina

"This book is dedicated to my Mom, Muriel Stanley - my friend, my confidante and the most amazing woman I know. Love you Mom".

Contents

Author's Note

• • •

"So . . . IF YOU COULD JUST complete this questionnaire that would be wonderful. Simply check off the boxes that apply – don't forget to elaborate on what 'other' means."

I get a bit excited because 'other' could mean a three-breasted cousin[1] or a late night trip across the U.S. border while being hidden in a trunk. 'Other' could mean an inheritance that was forfeited for love, or even a hidden sex addiction secretly tended to at an out-of-country treatment center.

Dear Reader,

This is my imaginary conversation with my parents, a questionnaire that might root out some crazy in the family, sprinkle a little weirdness on the family tree, put a little fun in the dysfunction.

Why? Why would I need to do this?

My childhood was too normal. You can't write a book without conflict . . . right? This is what I've believed for years and perhaps it has been the one thing that has stood in my way. It's my excuse.

My normal has been my albatross. I've actually felt some twisted jealousy toward those who have stories of personal or familial struggle. I think, "At least they have something to write about."

Yes . . . that does make me selfish.

I was born in the small town of Fairview, Alberta, Canada on a cold December day in 1964. I was small, but not dangerously small. My mom had smoked during the pregnancy, which is a surefire way to keep the

---

1 Not that there is anything wrong with that. #nojudgementhere

baby weight down. Don't judge my mom . . . it was 1964 and everyone smoked; even the doctor smoked *during* prenatal consultations. A little bit of trivia about our family doctor: In 1999, Dr. Snider went missing and was presumed dead. His colleague, Dr. Abraham Cooper, stood trial and was convicted of manslaughter in his death. Some say he was chopped up and tossed in a trunk – transported to an unknown location. Some say Dr. Snider faked his own death. Conspiracy theories abound.....I guess no one will ever know for sure.

Fairview was, and still remains, a small farming community in northwestern Alberta. To me it was the big, big city. The place where we went to watch movies, go Christmas shopping and go for fish and chips at the Chinese food restaurant. Why fish and chips? What kid do you know who likes Chinese food? What respectable Chinese food restaurant serves fish and chips? These are good questions . . .

But this isn't about missing or murdered doctors or crappy restaurants. It's about me: Judy, not anyone really famous or special in any way that might matter. Just a small town girl, writing a book and hoping that it means something to someone. Selfishly I hope that 'someone' is me.

Hello

● ● ●

I'M THE SECOND-BORN DAUGHTER, BORN fifteen months after my sister, Jessie. Not quite Irish Twins but close; close enough in looks to be twins. When I was young I told people we were one year apart because she was my idol, my confidante and my best friend. As I get older and more vain, I tell people we are two years apart. This isn't a surprising character flaw though; because I recently took a Narcissistic Personality Indicator Assessment online and scored rather high and, well . . . you know I wrote this book about myself.

Jessie and I ruled the roost until 1969 when my sister June was born. If you're noticing a trend with the names, you're correct. I tell people, "We were the Duggars[2] before the Duggars (with fewer kids)." Jessie, Judy, and June and, if that wasn't enough, we all had the middle initial 'L'.

Jaki Lin came along in 1973, born dangerously prematurely at twenty-six weeks. I had no clue that Mom was even pregnant. Jaki was a fighter! Only two pounds, she clung to life and was able to come home three months later. This was 1973, folks . . . things like this didn't happen. Babies born that small and premature didn't survive. I remember Mom coming into the house with Jaki bundled in her arms and Jaki making this weird noise. I was so excited! We were getting a cat!

It's important to note that Jaki was a perfect little thing and suffered very few after-effects of being so premature. So she had to take

---

2 An extremely large, religious Arkansas family who had their own television show until they were involved in a sex scandal.

kindergarten twice... no big deal. She just needed a little more time and has now caught up to the rest of us (except for her spelling . . . her spelling is atroshuss (atrocious).

We were the Stanley girls. Four vertically challenged girls with home cut hair, names that began with 'J' and middle names that began with 'L'.

My father, surrounded by an excessive amount of estrogen, chose to work in the oil patch, where he would be gone for days and weeks at a time. To add to the female contingent, Dad's mom, my grandmother, lived in a suite in the basement. No wonder he worked away all the time – he was literally surrounded by females. So . . . farming during the spring and summer, and hauling water for the oilfield industry in the winter became the cycle of our lives.

Left to our own devices for weeks on end, we grew extremely close to our mother.

This was my childhood, filled with playing in the canola swaths, riding our banana bikes into town on the heavily graveled roads, and straying miles away from home on a sunny afternoon with no worries, no concerns.

In 1977 our lives changed.

My father, an overachiever and Type A personality, suffered a massive coronary at thirty-nine years of age. As Mom drove us to school one morning after we missed the bus, Dad collapsed onto the floor at home with a crushing pain in his chest.

Mom returned home to find him lying on the floor with wee three-year-old Jaki sitting beside him. Miles away from the local hospital, this wasn't going to end well.

Except that it did.

Something amazing happened.

Dad was a private pilot and we owned a small Cessna 172. Owning an aircraft wasn't a rare occurrence in our community. I can recall at least three families who owned private planes. Thankfully, the runway on our property was always kept in perfect condition for those last-minute flights to get parts for the combine, or perhaps for just a fun ride in the evening. This time, that carefully groomed runway was to save Dad's life.

A call was made to our community health nurse (normally on call for immunizations and high fevers) and an air ambulance from Peace River was dispatched. The twin-engine aircraft landed on our private airstrip and taxied to the back door of our home, where Dad was quickly loaded for transport to Fairview – the same hospital where we'd all been born.

Dad coded in the air. Compressions were started. He survived, but our lives were changed forever.

Following open-heart surgery and a large farm sale at which Dad had to say goodbye to his beautiful airplane, farm equipment and the rich soil he'd tended so passionately, we moved away.

We were about to become little fish in a much larger pond. No plane. No farm. I would not be the fastest or the smartest. No one knew me and, worse . . . no one knew 'of' me.

Thus began my journey to create an identity in a world I'd only read about. Vancouver Island? I was a farm girl who'd only gone to three real movies in her lifetime. One of those movies was watched while eating chunks of garlic sausage and drinking from a large bottle of sprite that my dad had smuggled into the theatre. No popcorn for us! Nope! I also had no fashion sense at all and I dressed for comfort, not for style. I chewed my nails to the quick, I rarely wore shoes and the neighbor did my hair in her kitchen![3]

My dad had almost died, our farm was gone and I was separated from my friends.

This was going to be great!

So . . . as you read along you're going to ask yourself, "Is this book fact or fiction?"

---

3 She was NOT a hairdresser.

It's neither. It's based on fact, but vajazzled[4] up a bit. I've combed it, coifed it and littered it with rhinestones. Basically, I've polished a turd.

There are no three-breasted cousins, but there is depression, death and betrayal. Ultimately, this is a story about me and how my story is the story of so many my age: sometimes a comedy, sometimes a drama and, every so often, even a tragedy.

---

4 via Urban Dictionary: Vajazzle is to give the female pubic hair a sparkly makeover with crystals so as to enhance their appearance.

1. Just a SmallTown Girl

• • •

Inappropriate Me

● ● ●

"THINK BEFORE YOU SPEAK, JUDY," my parents would tell me.

"Look before you leap, Judy."

"If you can't say anything nice, don't say anything at all, Judy."

I tried so very hard to listen to their advice. Really, I did. They said that as I matured, my social 'filter' would mature as well. They also said I would grow. In both instances they were incorrect.

My earliest recorded inappropriate comment came at the expense of my uncle when I was about two years old. Apparently I had an aversion to being touched and when anyone outside of my magic circle tried to touch me, it would elicit a verbal response. In this case my uncle tried to pick me up. I told him to "fuck off." It was a 'Shock and Awwwww' moment. First there was shock that I had said something so terrible, and second it was "Awwwwww, isn't she cute?" Silly me. I assumed I could say things like that and get away with it.

You can't . . . and as I got older I struggled with breaking that bad habit. For the most part I have become someone you can take to a dinner party and not be afraid I will say something embarrassing, but every now and then there is a glimpse of that two-year-old:

"Why are we yelling? Is someone deaf?"

"Yes, Judy, someone is deaf," whispers my mortified mother as she turns, red-faced, to the group of ladies gathered in the kitchen.

"Hey you . . . you trying to steal my purse?" I say, laughing as I unlock myself from a hug from an elderly woman only to discover that she's a kleptomaniac and that my comment did not go unnoticed.

"Over my dead body!" I exclaim loudly, then realizing immediately that the woman had just lost her husband to a heart attack.

Honestly, I have been getting better. Baby steps.

Small Town

• • •

Like penny candy and glass pop bottles
bikes without helmets and corner stores
no shopping on Sunday
potluck dinners
everyone smiling

Like water from a spring
Clear, cold, fresh and pure
Everyone shares
Everyone tastes
We all drink together

Like sunshine on your face
And sweetness in your mouth
An endless stroll down memory lane
Fueled by hope
Small town happiness

Hooked on Farming

• • •

LIFE ON A FARM IS never, ever dull. There is no such thing as 'being bored' because if you dare utter those words you'll find yourself weeding a garden or mowing an acre or two of grass. We were left to our own devices quite often – even more so during harvest. The evenings, when both Mom and Dad were out on the field combining and transporting canola, meant playing without rules or a bedtime. Some nights, if a warm wind was blowing, Mom and Dad would both stay out 'til the wee hours, taking advantage of the perfect harvest conditions. My sisters and I took advantage as well.

It was during one of these marathon combine sessions that my ten-year-old self got into a bit of trouble.

I think I've mentioned before that my father had a water trucking company serving the oilfield. During the winter he hauled water to rigs and camps and during the summer and fall he farmed. When the summer season rolled around, the water tanks were removed from the trucks and left to rest on large metal drums in the front yard. Lined up, they were quite an impressive display and so much fun to play on!

I know, I know. We shouldn't have been playing on the empty tanks but honestly, what ten-year-old could resist? They resembled submarines with metal ladders and a hinged porthole cover on the top. Up and down the tanks my sister Jessie and I would climb, sometimes imagining that we could leap from one to the other. (We never did. We weren't *that* crazy.)

One of my favorite things to do was to sit on the top of the tank and slide off the glossy-painted, slippery metal into the long grass. Even resting on the steel drums, the tanks weren't elevated enough to be dangerously high, and the long grass that circled the barrels underneath the tanks resembled golden, gentle waves. I never once thought about the metal hooks welded to the side of the tank where the hoses were stored. They made a 'U' shape and came out from the tank approximately eight inches. I screamed with delight as I slid off of the tank, immediately turning around and climbing the metal ladder to slide off again, always managing to avoid the sharp hooks.

Until that time I didn't miss the big metal hook.

In fact, I impaled myself on the sharp piece of steel and hung there for a moment. Shock on my face, I looked up at my sister Jessie, who wore an expression of horror and then one of worry with the thought that "Mom is going to blame me because I'm the oldest and supposed to be in charge."

Time passed slowly and I can recall wondering how on earth I was going to remove myself from this 'thing' without doing more damage. I didn't have to think about it long because, as I leaned forward, I managed to free myself, gently slipping off the hook that was now slick with my blood. I tumbled into the long grass, standing up quickly like a gymnast who had stuck her landing.

I didn't cry and I didn't scream. I just began walking toward the house, the adrenaline blocking the pain from piercing my consciousness.

The hook had caught me high on the back of my thigh and actually pierced my butt cheek. I could tell it was fairly deep because fat from my butt was protruding out the gash, puking out the edges like cottage cheese. The question was, "Was it important enough to call my mom off the field? Did we dare get on the radio and alert her to the potential for a quick trip to the community nurse?"

Tetanus? Didn't even think about tetanus.

As Jessie and I conferred, it was determined (by Jessie) that I was going to live and that we definitely shouldn't call Mom off of the field. It wasn't bleeding and I was still breathing so, according to our limited knowledge of emergency medicine, there was no reason to panic.

We cleaned it with Mercurochrome and placed a band-aid over the deep puncture in my thigh. Now it was time to get our stories straight. We definitely were *not* playing on the water tanks. We definitely had *not* left our younger siblings in the house while we played on the water tanks.

We turned on the television and tried to focus on the *Wonderful World of Disney*, with one nervous eye on the front window watching for the lights of the combine to round the corner.

Nearing 10 p.m., the lumbering grain-eating machine came into the yard. Still awake and with my leg throbbing, I explained the sanitized version of events to Mom and then showed her my thigh.

The look on her face said it all. It was bad. The tissue around the gash had begun to bruise and it looked ugly. A little concerned at this point, I told her the truth about how the injury occurred and prepared myself for the worst.

I shouldn't have been worried. Of course she didn't get angry. She gave me a hug and we shared a nervous, relieved laugh that it hadn't been worse. Years later she shared how guilty she felt about having to be out on the field for those long hours and that I had got injured. I never played on the water tanks again (well . . . I never slid off the top again).

I Can Fly!

• • •

I CAN'T RECALL EXACTLY HOW old I was when it happened. I wouldn't be surprised if I somehow might have suffered a brain injury from the impact. All I know is that I hit the wall hard . . . and I never looked at life the same way again.

As a child, I used to consider myself a bit of a tomboy. In retrospect, the only thing I had in common with a tomboy was that I rarely wore dresses and my hair was cropped short like a boy. Oh yeah . . . I also had a filthy mouth like a sailor. Despite having many of the tomboy trappings, I was scared of bugs, bears, dirt, loud things, fast things, dead things . . . I played tough but would rely on my very fast short legs to get me out of a bind.

Anyhow . . . I've mentioned before that I grew up on a farm, but not a real farm as one might imagine when thinking of a farm.

It was a grain farm.

We grew grain.

I never had to go gather fresh eggs in the morning or feed the cattle. I never had to milk a cow (although there was a brief time that we were encouraged to milk our lone goat, which, in hindsight, I'm certain that my father intended to be our 'gateway' goat and lead to a genuine interest in animal husbandry. Never happened).

The entire experience was gross. The goat didn't want to stand still and the milk tasted funny. Blech!

It was a failed experiment and one day the goat was gone. Poof! (Don't get melodramatic. I'm certain the goat was given to a neighbor.)

Like I said, we grew up on a farm but we are only entitled to label our experience 'Farm-lite'.

So I think you have the picture.

The day *it* happened was very, very cold. A frigid winter day when my sisters and I were house-bound with only Channel 13 (CTV) to keep us company. That channel was so fuzzy that we could barely make out the grey shapes of the Skipper and Gilligan and no amount of tinfoil on the rabbit ears was going to improve things.

Frustrated, we turned it off and we dispersed to our individual spaces to read or play.

I didn't want to read. I wanted to take my brand new Krazy Karpet and fly down a hillside like they advertised on television:

"Krazy Karpet is the new space-age slider! Safe, lightweight, easy to handle . . . wild! Pilot *your* Krazy Karpet over any surface!"

Each of us girls had received a Krazy Karpet for Christmas and I couldn't wait to try it out. But that day it was too cold to go slip-sliding on my Krazy Karpet and we were nowhere near a hillside with enough slope to slip.

Hmmmmm. We *did* have a basement and we did have stairs and the commercial *did* say that I could pilot my Krazy Karpet over *any* surface.

The daylight basement was accessible by a flight of stairs that extended from the back entry landing area to the entrance of the mother in law suite downstairs. My memory is a bit foggy but I imagine there were probably twenty highly-glossed, painted steps.

Seemed like enough steps for a nice ride.

I peeled the protective sticky label off of my new Krazy Karpet and unrolled it carefully. My short arms tried to flatten out the plastic, but my child-size wingspan was insufficient. Finally I sat down on the end of the Karpet, flattening it sufficiently so that the front part curled up into my lap, begging me to slip my fingers through the small oval 'handle'.

I looked just like the kids on the commercial!

Oooooooh, I wanted to try it soooooo badly!

I called my older sister to join me at the top of the stairs. "I'm going to ride my Krazy Karpet down the stairs," I said excitedly.

Jessie's face lit up and to this day I wonder if she knew what was going to happen and simply chose to play along.

There was nothing else required. I had my older sister's implied consent. This launch was a 'go'.

I was going to pilot my Karrrrpettttt!

I shuffled the Karpet forward inch by inch and finally I was perched on the top step, the front end of the plastic curled out and back towards me, my two small hands with fingernails bitten to the quick tucked into the sharp oval cutout.

I leaned forward.

It began slowly at first, my body making contact with the top step, then the next, then the next and now I am FLYING through the air, stair after stair after stair!

The wall came so quickly I had no time to bail. You know that stupid joke where they ask, "What went through the bug's head after he hit the windshield?"

Answer: "Its brain."

BAM! That was me.

My little body launched headfirst from the final step straight into the drywall at the bottom of the stairs and I crumpled into a pile.

For a moment I was stunned.

I hadn't considered the wall placement, nor the physics and trajectory involved with the slide down the stairs.

Groaning, I began to extricate myself from the sheet of hard plastic, the shiny surface now branded with scuffmarks and paint rubs from the basement stairs.

Jessie was looking at me worriedly, probably wondering how much trouble she'd be in if I didn't survive.

She was the oldest . . . she was in charge.

Standing up, I checked myself over carefully.

No blood.

No broken bones.

"Are you okay?" said Jessie, her face(s) only inches away from mine. I didn't dare tell her that at this very moment there was two of her looking me in the eyes.

I nodded carefully; not wanting to let on that my bell had been rung hard – very hard.

I think she knew that I was having some difficulty focusing because she helped roll up that Krazy Karpet and we went back upstairs.

Childhood for a farm kid was like that . . . even for those of us who practiced Farm-lite. It was survival of the fittest or luckiest or whatever.

For some of us it was riding a Krazy Karpet down the stairs; for others it was knife throwing competitions in the back yard.

We survived.

Are You a Narc?

● ● ●

"AH YOU OR AH YOU naht a nahck?" Remember that line from the movie, *The Heat?* The heavy Boston accent as the dude asked Sandra Bullock if she were a narc?

Been there, done that.

No, I haven't been a narc but I have been asked to be one and have been asked if I was indeed a 'narc.'

As I mentioned in my introduction, our family relocated from a Northern Alberta farm to a home on Vancouver Island with the speed normally reserved for concealing a teenage pregnancy. We moved because Dad was convinced he was going to kick the bucket and he wanted to move us somewhere, 'nicer' and 'gentler' and closer to my mom's parents. I'm certain he imagined himself sitting in a chair on the deck, looking out at the ocean, a blanket tucked around his knees. Following his heart attack and bypass surgery he was convinced that he would suffer the same fate as his own father and die a young man. He was only forty years old.

We were extremely 'small town.' I might already mentioned that I'd only been to a movie theatre three times in my life, and you will recall that one of those times Dad smuggled in a roll of garlic sausage and a glass bottle[5] of pop. We sat in the back row so the lingering scent of garlic was somewhat contained. I was so 'small town' I wasn't even embarrassed.

---

5 No plastic back then.

The family moved in late spring, our teachers giving us our final report cards early; they could do that sort of thing in a small rural school. This meant that we would have a longer than normal summer vacation – an opportunity to become acclimatized to our new world.

It was amazing! The sun, the sandy beaches, the cedar trees, the PAVED ROADS! I fell in love immediately and it wasn't long before I was riding my bike back and forth to nearby Shawnigan Lake to sneak into the country club for a swim. I even got a summer job working at a local tomato farm because . . . well . . . deep down I was still a farm girl and I felt I'd have a leg up on the competition because of my specialized skill set.

Little did I know that no one was competing with me for a job at the tomato farm – partly because of the heat and humidity and partly because of the spiders. Little did I know that Vancouver Island spiders are much, much larger than northern Alberta spiders and the greenhouse created perfect conditions to grow monster arachnids. Did I mention that I was terrified of spiders?

It was like something out of a nightmare. Creepy crawlies were everywhere and the smell! To this day the smell of a tomato plant brings back memories. Combine it with the fact that the owner thought it was all right to 'lift me up' to pick the tomatoes instead of letting me use the ladder and I lasted less than a month. I didn't tell my parents about him lifting me up because (a) I wasn't certain if Dad's heart would take it and (b) we northern-raised folk solved problems (like a strange man inappropriately touching a thirteen-year-old) differently than the relaxed Island folk.

Trust me.

Finally it was August and a new school year was right around the corner. A new school! New people! New friends! Apparently it was called a 'middle school' because it housed only three grades: eight, nine and ten. What was the most exciting part of this new adventure? Each grade contained levels dividing up the students according to where they best fit academically. Finally I would be housed with my own kind! Of course I was assigned Grade 8A.

The first day of school arrived and my sister and I made our way to the bus stop. I was wearing a brand new pair of Big Blue brand wide-leg jeans, platform shoes, a plaid shirt and a corduroy blazer. My hair was cut in a Dorothy Hamill wedge and I'd used some of my sister's eyeliner. This was 1978 and I was thirteen years old.

My sister was much more 'chill' about the first day of school. First of all, she was assigned class 9B, which was interpreted as being smart, but not nerd-smart like me. She didn't wear brand-new clothes but instead opted for something pre-worn and casual. I don't think she even used a new binder, but carried one that had already weathered a year of use. She was going to fit in if it killed her!

Walking to the bus stop I was very nervous and excited! I loved change. I loved a challenge. I was going to *rock* this new school!

As the bus pulled up in front of the campus, the school appeared massive and there were so many students! The building had long ago out-grown itself, necessitating the use of half a dozen 'portable' classrooms.

My mind was blown!

As I sat in my 8A orientation class, I heard over the loudspeaker, "Judy Stanley and Jessie Stanley please go to the principal's office immediately."

Puzzled at first, but then understanding that the principal was probably going to welcome us personally to the new school and applaud our previous academic standing, I quickly made my way to the office.

My new jeans swished and my stiff corduroy blazer made that delightful corduroy sound. My hair bounced and swayed as I walked, just as it was intended.

Jessie was already seated in the cramped office and she looked worried. I sat down beside her and with a big stupid smile I reached over the desk and shook the white-haired principal's hand.

"Hi there!" I said excitedly.

He was surprised and maybe a little shocked at first, but then he smiled back while pumping my hand in return.

Jessie rolled her eyes.

"Welcome to George Bonner. I wanted to welcome you both to the school and let you know that I'm here for you if you need any help," he said.

I knew it! Wow! What a welcoming school!

"My door is always open and I wanted to let you both know that you can come and talk to me any time, especially if you see something strange or out of place on campus."

Strange? I wonder what he thinks we might see that is strange? Maybe he's talking about skunks. I had smelled a skunk when I entered the school an hour earlier.

Jessie leaned over and whispered, "Let's go. *Now.*"

Shocked at her lack of manners, I mean . . . this isn't how we were raised, I stayed seated.

"What might you be referring to?" I asked politely, wishing that I'd brought my new binder filled with blank, ruled paper in order to make notes.

The principal looked at me with a curious expression, almost as if to say, "Did you just fall off the turnip truck?"

Jessie grabbed my arm and pulled me to my feet, walking out of the office. "Sorry! Can't help you," she said sweetly but firmly, and dragged me from the room.

"Jesus, Jessie! Do you have to be so rude?" I said as we entered the hallway. Immediately I felt badly because I'd said "Jesus" and my limited religious upbringing had taught me not to use the Lord's name in vain. "Don't say the word Jesus unless you're talking to Him," Dad would say. Saying the name in any other situation was apparently bad ju-ju.

"Are you an idiot? Isn't it enough that you *look* like a narc?" she said with her superior older-sister tone.

"A narc? What's a narc?" Clearly I was confused.

"A narc! Someone who tattles when they see kids using narcotics! Duh!" Jessie said, rolling her expertly-lined green eyes. I had barely mastered brushing my teeth daily, whereas Jessie was a tampon-wearing, mascara-wielding, purse-toting young woman.

Clearly my hours watching *The Beachcombers* and fuzzy Walt Disney movies on one of two channels that we managed to tune into using rabbit ears and tinfoil hadn't prepared me for my new life on Vancouver Island.

Horrified, I responded, "You mean <gasp> smokers?"

The frustration on Jessie's face now was replaced with compassion and pity. She spoke very slowly. "No Judy, I'm talking about drugs like marijuana."

I sucked in a breath quickly, causing myself to choke. I managed to sputter, "You mean . . . pot? Kids our age smoke pot?"

My mind was spinning[6] and I struggled to regain my composure.

Speaking softly now, Jessie tried to explain. "He (the principal) thought we were an easy mark. He wanted us to do his dirty work for him. If we'd agreed to do it, to become his informants, we'd never make friends. We'd never fit in."

So began my year of transformation from a naïve country bumpkin to a (still naïve) teenager living on Vancouver Island. If not for the quick actions of my sis, I would have alienated my peers in ways my corduroy blazer and wedge haircut could not.

I am not a narc.

---

6 If my head had been spinning, no doubt my Dorothy Hamill hair would have swung effortlessly as well.

Through a Haze of Smoke

• • •

WITHIN MONTHS OF RELOCATING TO Vancouver Island I had immersed myself in the cultural underbelly and had begun to express myself. I knew what I needed to do to fit in.

I smoked pot. I smoked a lot of pot. Ironic, isn't it? That same newbie that the principal wanted to be a narc and rat out her friends would now be the subject of a narc. I smoked on the way to the bus stop, I smoked at lunch hour and I smoked on the way home. The little girl with the Dorothy Hamill wedge haircut now had long hair past her shoulders and expertly applied makeup. I was also skinny beyond belief, eating for breakfast only a bowl of Raisin Bran with barely enough milk to moisten the flakes. I followed that hearty breakfast with a hundred sit-ups and an hour-long bike ride over winding roads. At this point I weighed eighty-seven pounds and could fit my hand under my rib cage. I thought I looked beautiful and for the first time in my life I felt like I was in control.

I knew I had an eating disorder but the sense of control I had over my body was intoxicating. I could manage to function on less than five hundred calories a day!

I was walking a tightrope. It was just a matter of time.

Strangely enough, my grades didn't suffer terribly. I held onto my Grade 8A privileges *and* managed to fit into my new school. I straddled the line between good girl and bad girl.

Car rides to Victoria with six kids in a Honda Civic hatchback or bonfires on the beach smoking myself into a sleepy, dopey buzz . . . it was the late 1970s and I was no longer a farm girl from the sleepy hamlet of Worsley.

I'd lost my connection to that small town. The canola swathes and bike rides into town on the thickly-graveled roads were becoming a distant memory. My life now was filled with a kaleidoscope of parties and pot and Pink Floyd.

Remember, I was thirteen years old when I began Grade 8. A mature thirteen but still thirteen, with the farm girl naiveté that couldn't be erased. I was pretending to understand the world I was living in, but it was all pot smoke and mirrors on my part.

I recall being confused. I wanted so desperately to belong and to blend in, but I didn't want to cross *the* line. Pot was harmless, flirtation with boys was fun and I had cultivated a bitch persona that made me feel untouchable. I was the cool girl who brandished her metal barrettes when someone was searching for something to use to hot-knife hash oil.

I was operating through a haze of smoke.

Happy Dolphins

• • •

ONE SATURDAY NIGHT WHEN I was about fourteen years old I returned from a date with my eighteen-year-old boyfriend (what was I thinking?!), dug through the medicine cabinet (that's what they were called back then) until I found something stronger than Aspirin and then I swallowed them – all fifteen of them.

Then I went to bed.

It wasn't an impulsive act.

You see, for weeks up until the very moment I opened the door of the medicine cabinet, I'd asked myself, "What do I have to look forward to?" and each time I managed to come up with something. That morning, for the very first time, I hadn't been able to think of anything. Nothing had presented itself throughout the day and therefore I found myself in this most unusual position.

I'd mastered the body control and had dieted myself into skin and bones. I'd snagged a boyfriend who was in high school. I'd been the good girl, then the wild child, and now I had nothing left.

I tell people that I craved the feeling of being 'special' but whatever I did, whatever I put myself through, didn't live up to the expectations. I was never going to feel special enough.

I know now that it was a nonsensical thing to do, but I wasn't thinking clearly at the time. I took the pills and went to bed. I am so very grateful that, after some poking and prodding by my sister[7], I woke up the next morning.

---

7 Thankfully we still shared a room.

After groggily telling my family what I'd done, I was immediately dressed and taken to the 'therapist' neighbor for counseling. The neighbors were a yuppie professional couple who were building a home in the next subdivision. Their yard was a construction site and their home was partially completed. I have no recollection of how my parents knew them, or knew of them, but they became my therapist/counselor for the next little while as I tried to work through what my issues were and why I thought killing myself was a good idea.

I recall sitting in their living room that morning, drinking God-awful herbal tea and crying. The husband, who wore cardigans and wire-rimmed glasses, helped me to understand that I was suffering from depression – and that depression doesn't equal crazy. I'd gone through massive stress and trauma over the past year: Dad's health, moving away from the farm, the culture shock and the need to fit in with the new life. It was understandable that I was having difficulty.

Over time, I eventually began to feel better, but 'it' would not go away forever. Always below the surface, like a sleeping giant, depression would rear its ugly head again.

Why am I even mentioning it?

Depression is something that I've overcome, but it's also something that I will wear forever.

Is it a flaw? I don't think so. Just because my brain plays Jedi mind tricks on me occasionally doesn't make me a freak. It just means that the 'force' is a little stronger with me . . .

'Happy Dolphins' has become a mantra of sorts – a declaration of happiness. Just because I'm not suffering depression doesn't mean that I'm always a beacon of light. I think we all need to work hard at being happy. And Happy Dolphins (can't you just picture their cuteness?) make *me* happy.

So, it pains me to say, I guess I'm not perfect. But then again . . . who is?

2. The Cat Came Back

· · ·

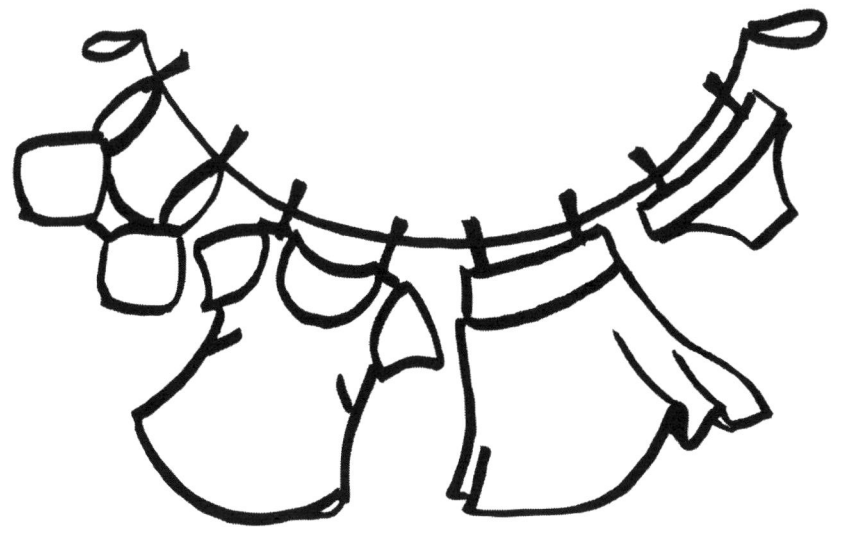

Hey Baby

• • •

IN 1980 WE LOADED UP the moving vans and relocated to Dawson Creek, approximately two hours southwest of where our family farm had been located.

After three years and three grades of school on Vancouver Island I was going to be back in the North; a little older but so much wiser. I was no longer going to be the naïve newcomer. Instead I was the 'worldly girl' from Vancouver Island – or so I imagined.

This might be a good time to bring you up to date on the health of my father. As you might recall we'd originally moved to Vancouver Island because he was convinced he was going to die of heart disease. Surprisingly, his health flourished, but his mood did not. He disliked Vancouver Island because it was wet, gray and rainy during the winter. Not long after we arrived on the Island he was back in Alberta looking for a new 'non-farmer'[8] career.

After discovering his niche in the oilfield road and lease building area, Dad commuted back and forth between Northern Alberta and Northern BC to Vancouver Island. Mom, my sisters and I remained on the Island during that time.

Three years passed.

As one can imagine, he grew weary of the long commute and the decision was made to move closer to where his work was located. The choices? Grande Prairie or Dawson Creek.

---

8 Farming had proved to be too stressful.

Dawson Creek was a smaller, farming community and perhaps was the more comfortable choice over Grande Prairie – a city that was growing exponentially and 'booming' in the glory days of the oil and gas industry.

I often wonder what my life would have been like if we'd settled in Grande Prairie.

I always felt out of place in Dawson Creek, especially at school. Surrounded by kids who had grown up with the same friends, I was the outsider. The cliquey nature of my classmates was indicative of the northern mentality, and was very similar to the school I had attended in Worsley as a child. I don't blame them for not being welcoming.

Fortunately I'm an extrovert and couldn't possibly survive unless surrounded by people and activity. I also welcomed the opportunity to once again reinvent myself, abandoning the persona I'd embodied on Vancouver Island and embracing the familiar 'northern gal, small town' persona.

I graduated in 1982 with so-so grades and got a job at a local bank. During my last year of high school I'd met my future husband and it wasn't long before an engagement ring appeared on my finger.

Everything was going according to plan. That is, until I got pregnant. In September of 1982, at the tender age of 17, I discovered that some types of birth control are not one hundred per cent effective and not only was I pregnant, but I was almost three months pregnant. In my defence, I have a weird cycle that dances around the calendar landing on random dates and surprising me, so I really had no clue that anything was amiss.

Terrified and disappointed with myself, I told Bob and then went to inform my mom of my big news.

I used to joke about the fact that, "If I had stayed in Worsley I would've married my cousin in high school and had babies," but here I was, pregnant at 17.

Thankfully (can I use that word and not have everyone hating on me?), the universe must have conferred and determined that it would be "crazy to let this girl have a baby right now" and I suffered a miscarriage two days later. Armed with a prescription for birth control pills and a healthy respect for my young and fertile reproductive system, I left the hospital determined not to place my implicit trust in any type of birth control ever again.

I married Bob in February of 1984: a huge wedding with approximately three hundred people in attendance. My sisters were my bridesmaids, wearing red taffeta tea-length dresses and carrying bouquets of red and white carnations. My dress was incredibly ugly (No, I'm not exaggerating; it was ugly.) and I wore a white cowboy-style hat with a big tulle bow that cascaded down the back. We ate our reception meal of turkey, potatoes, cabbage roles and perogies against a backdrop of streamers and silver hearts created out of tinfoil. Our first dance was to the theme song from Dr. Zhivago: *Lara's Theme*. The piano was out of tune and some keys were broken. When the pianist got to the "love" part of "Somewhere my love," the note was sharp and tinny. Ughhhhhh . . .

I recently googled *Lara's Theme*. Now I know why some people were confused when we took to the dance floor: The song is about death and lost love.

I can't forget to mention the wedding photos. There's a reason why I have no wedding pictures hanging in my home. In an attempt to save money, our photos were taken in front of a yellow/gold set of drapes at a neighbor's house. No one, I mean *no one*, looks good against that backdrop.

So began my life as a wife. I remember the tears as I said goodbye to my parents after the gift opening, because I had never spent a lot of time away from home. Hey, I was nineteen years old – do you blame me? Who knows who they are at nineteen years of age? There should be a law against getting married before age twenty-five! I had such skewed expectations of myself and my relationship. Raised in a traditional household where my mother stayed home and my father worked, I felt that I had to overcompensate and do it all – work and raise children.

My first wedding anniversary was celebrated with a positive pregnancy test and Amy was born in September of 1985.

You know the saying, it was the best of times and it was also the worst.

I not only was trying to do it all, I was alienating those who could help me – namely my mom. I didn't want her to think I was failing and I didn't want my husband to think I couldn't handle being a new mom.

The months passed in a blur, and I sank into one of the deepest depressions I've ever suffered.

Broken

• • •

THE BOOK WAS FLYING FROM my hand before I realized I'd picked it up. The large window – original to our cute but tiny starter home – reacted with the force. The interior panel resembled cracked ice, the layers and layers of paint acting like glue, keeping it from falling apart entirely and sprinkling the carpet with glass.

I was nauseated.

I was scared.

Nothing I could dream up could sufficiently explain away a broken window.

I tripped? Hardly.

A bird hit the window? Not likely.

No.

Relief washed over me.

I shivered.

I'm crazy. Am I crazy?

Is that a question?

No . . . the broken window has to be a big clue that something is wrong with me.

Right?

I begin to cry and only then realize that I'm not alone.

Oh. Amy.

Her little tear-stained face was red and she looked confused. Standing in her crib, wee hands clinging to the railing, her oversized cloth diaper drooping – obviously saturated.

Fucking cloth diapers. How many times had I poked myself with a pin while trying to wrestle this square wad of cotton flannelette into something resembling a diaper? What was I trying to prove by using cloth diapers? A diaper pail in the bathroom does not proclaim, "I am Mother Fucking Earth."

Hardly.

I could hear her breathing, her worried eyes searching my face for something. Reassurance? Comfort?

Not yet a toddler, Amy had always been wise beyond her . . . months?

I was a failure.

I couldn't satisfy her.

She never slept.

My tears increased, my face scrunching up into a truly 'ugly' cry. I was sobbing, shoulders heaving, barely able to catch my breath. I slid down the wall until I was sitting on the floor, knees against my chest. My post-baby tummy and breasts were sandwiched together – my five-foot frame made it difficult to wrap my short arms around my knees. I sat awkwardly.

The unbearable sadness I'd been feeling for months was leaking out of every pore like a horrible cheap perfume.

Do you remember the perfume Jean Naté? I hated that perfume.

This paralyzing sadness leaching out of my skin was best described as having "undertones of disappointment with top notes of failure to meet expectations."

It's difficult to describe what the weight of sadness feels like.

"How do you feel, Judy?"

"Funny you should ask! Well, I feel like I have a suit of heavy armor (steel, not aluminum) with a scuba diving weight belt wrapped around the middle. Every few days or weeks, another weight is added until finally I crumple into a heap."

"Oh Judy, you exaggerate so!"

I could hardly stand it anymore.

This wasn't living.

It had overtaken me and now everyone is going to find out because I broke the stupid window.

"Why did you throw the book?"

"Because I was pissed off."

"Why were you pissed off?"

"I'm always pissed off."

My textbook version of baby blues had morphed into a black cloud so heavy and thick that I could hardly breathe!

I wanted to tell everyone to "FUCK RIGHT OFF" but getting angry took more energy than I had.

I was too sad to be angry.

I was completely and utterly empty.

"Judy . . . you broke the fucking window? How did you break the fucking window? Are you crazy? Who breaks their own fucking window?"

The tears had stopped falling and my eyes were now red and puffy, my sleeve wet with snot, my face flushed.

The crib squeaked.

Right. I wasn't by myself.

I turned my head.

My wise little girl was sitting Buddha-like on her massive soggy diaper, leaning her forehead against the wooden crib slats, staring at me, her breathing steady.

She loves me. She hates me. She needs me.

She's smarter than I am.

She can read my mind.

Maybe she's thinking, "Whatcha doin' Mum?"

No . . . she's probably wishing, "How do I arrange a do-over? I didn't sign up for this shit."

I was wishing the same thing.

The sadness had snuck up on me, clinging to me bit by bit, like mold on a wheel of cheese.

I angered easily, had no motivation, couldn't think, couldn't sleep, couldn't lose the baby weight, felt like a failure . . . I could go on and on.

The kicker?

My kid WOULD NOT FUCKING SLEEP, either.

Looking at her, I whispered, "What do you want from me?"

I didn't know what to do.

I didn't know what to think.

I knew I loved her.

I knew I did.

Right?

I knew.

I loved *her*, but this mother thing was really difficult; more difficult than I could ever imagine.

I didn't even have ownership of my brain any longer. My thoughts were crazy thoughts. My dreams were crazy dreams.

I knew I should be happy.

"Judy . . . don't 'should' yourself!"

It makes me giggle. I heard that once, "Don't *should* yourself."

I guess it's true. Shoulda, woulda, coulda. It rhymes . . . kind of.

"When the bough breaks, the cradle will fall." Now that is some sick shit. What kind of brain comes up with stuff like that? I mean, have you read the lyrics? The goddamn cradle falls! The baby FALLS! OUT OF A TREE!

Seriously?

I guess it's the tone we use. Like, when we speak to a dog, it doesn't really matter what we say but rather, how we say it.

I could look at my dog and say in a loving voice, "Aren't you a little bastard? Who is my little bastard?" and my dog would wag his tail with happiness. He doesn't care what I say, just how I say it.

Babies must be the same.

How long have I been sitting here?

It's getting dark out.

Shit. The window really is broken.

Nothing has changed.

Maybe it has? I feel like something has shifted, something inside me has broken free.

Maybe just a little bit?

Oh Amy, I sure love you but holy shit . . . no one told me it would be this hard.

No one said that my dreams would take me on a journey of vivid, brilliant colors and feelings. Some nights I wake up afraid of what I'd seen in the depths of my imagination.

Can you smell a dream?

Some nights I swear my dreams smell horrible – like dead-body horrible or maggots-eating-flesh horrible.

Decay.

Is this what it feels like to be dead?

She loves me. She needs me.

Don't call me crazy. It isn't kind to use that term.

Deep breaths . . . deep breaths.

Who am I gonna call? What do I say?

I'm sad?

I'm hurting?

I'm scared?

I broke a fucking window?

Judy! It could have been worse! What if you'd . . .

Hurt someone? Hurt myself? Hurt her?

I hate *myself*, but I don't hate her.

She loves me. She needs me.

Big. Blue. Eyes.

She has the most beautiful blue eyes and she's staring at me right now.

I lean closer.

I can feel her milky baby breath warm upon my face.

What is she thinking?

Does she think in words yet? No, she thinks in feelings.

Hungry. Happy. Sleepy .

No. For Christ's sake, never *ever* sleepy.

What feeling does she have right now?

Pity? Does she pity me?

Okay, let's think about this.

I need some help.
I must get some help.
I don't want to feel this way any longer.
I need to tell someone.

I look away, staring contest over. Amy wins.
Oh Amy, how did you get so smart?
You love me and you need me.
I love you and I need you.

After the Rain

• • •

YOU KNOW THAT SMELL THAT permeates the air after a summer rainstorm? You open the doors and windows and the breeze carries the freshly laundered air throughout your home. You breathe in deeply, feeling it make its way to every part of your being?

That's what I felt after months of medication and therapy for postpartum depression.

After I threw the book through the window and finally sought help, my doctor responded quickly with anti-depressants and a referral to a psychologist. I was forced to face my demons and ask for help, one of the most difficult things for someone of my nature to request.

Asking for help was admitting failure . . . right?

Wrong. I needed to learn that asking for help was exactly what I needed to do to keep my sanity and help me to recover from this dark place I'd settled into over the months.

I realized how angry I had been and was surprised to learn that anger can be just as prolific as despondency when diagnosing depression. In my case, unreasonable anger is something that I recognize and have to act on quickly if I want to stem the tide of depression before it takes over completely.

I was learning. After each depressive episode I was learning how to live with this beast that seemed to climb out from the closet and smother me when I least expected it.

3. When the Bough Breaks

• • •

Shit Happens

• • •

AFTER THREE MONTHS OF BREASTFEEDING, which I *hated*, I gave it up and moved to formula. I know why I disliked breastfeeding: I was a nervous, uninformed mother who didn't reach out for support or guidance. Had I reached out for assistance, the breastfeeding might have worked out more positively. Amy was a very fussy baby and a prolific 'puker.' You never knew when she would projectile puke. Nowadays she would have been diagnosed as lactose intolerant or something of that nature, but back in the day there were only three ways to feed her: breast milk, Similac[9] or Enfalac.

We settled on Enfalac in the powdered form. Measured carefully and mixed with sterilized, boiled water, bottles were made each morning for the day. Powdered formula was less expensive than canned, liquid formula and we were on a tight budget.

One of the problems with powdered formula is that if it isn't mixed very carefully it can cause constipation. Have you ever been around a constipated baby? They scream, they cry, they pull their knees up to their chest and seem inconsolable.

Part of the new 'me' meant asking for help and thankfully my mom lived nearby.

"Mom, Amy's constipated! What should I do?" I asked frantically over the telephone.

---

9 Similac and Enfalac were the only baby formula brands available during that time – options were limited.

Mom was very quick with advice. "Mix one tablespoon of corn starch into each bottle and shake well. Try that for a day and it should loosen her up."

I had an entire box of corn starch that was normally only used for thickening gravy, so I began immediately, adding it to each prepared bottle and shaking well.

The next morning Amy was still in agony. Try as hard as she could, there was no way her bowels were going to move.

Near tears, I called Mom for help. "Mom, Amy's still constipated! What should I do? Should I increase the corn starch?"

There was a brief pause on the telephone and then I heard, "Corn starch? Corn starch! Oh my goodness, it should have been corn syrup! No wonder she can't poop!"

I dumped the prepared bottles out and dashed down to the drug store to purchase a baby suppository. It took two to get things moving and finally Amy was back to herself again: fussy eater and crappy sleeper, but she pooped!

Poor Amy and poor Mom. I don't think Mom ever forgot (and I haven't let her).

Boy Meets World

● ● ●

ON A HOT SUMMER EVENING in August 1988 we welcomed Matthew into the world.

I was placed on anti-depressants before I was discharged from the hospital and spent the first three weeks staying at Mom and Dad's house because the medication made me really sleepy and there was no guarantee I'd wake up to feed Matthew in the night.

No need to worry. Matthew slept through the night within the first month, sometimes sleeping as many as nine hours at a time. The first time it happened I woke up in a panic, thinking he'd suffocated in his sleep, only to find him sleeping peacefully.

I needed a Matthew in my life. I don't think I could have survived another Amy. I didn't even attempt to breastfeed Matthew because of my daily dose of anti-depressants.

Life was good. I was feeling healthy and my mind hadn't dragged me down into that dark place again.

Thank God for medication.

Lice Aren't Nice

● ● ●

I WORKED THE WIDE-TOOTHED COMB through her waist-length hair with a minimum of resistance. A light spritz of No More Tears/No More Tangles was the key to a drama and tear-free hair combing experience with my eight-year-old daughter.

Out of the corner of my eye I saw something move down the length of parted hair and I quickly placed a finger overtop of it before it could get away. Placing it in the palm of my hand I looked it over carefully. My goodness! It was a teeny, tiny bug.

"Bob! Can you come here for a second?" I had no clue what type of bug it was and it was strange that it was crawling in her hair. Bob would no doubt be able to identify the grayish-brown bug.

I held my hand out in front of his face. "This was crawling in Amy's hair. Do you know what it is?"

Bob examined the bug thoughtfully before squeezing it between his thumb and forefinger, ending its life. He then wrapped it in a tissue and flushed it down the toilet.

He began to wash his hands vigorously under the tap in the sink of the ensuite bathroom, a room that barely fit a single person, much less the two of us plus Amy and a stool.

"It's . . . ummm . . . it's lice," he whispered as he pushed past me, flattening his body against the door frame, creating as much distance as he could between himself and his daughter.

Certain that I had misheard him, I said, "What? WHAT is it?" my voice pitching higher as I spoke.

Bob met my gaze, glanced at Amy and then quickly looked back at me and shook his head as if to say, "I'll tell you later" and left the room.

"What is it, Mum?" Amy asked, looking up from her book.

"It's nothing, sweetheart. Now let's get this hair braided and you off to bed so you can finish reading your book." I quickly twisted and turned her hair over and under until a nice tight French braid rested down the middle of her back.

After tucking both Amy and our little boy Matthew into their beds, I retreated to the living room to find out what Bob had been talking about earlier.

"It's lice. That bug was a lice bug. Not a nit, not a gnat, not an egg, but a bug. An actual lice bug. We have louse in the house." As Bob said this, he reached up to scratch his own head in solidarity.

"SHE HAS LICE?! How can she have lice? I keep her hair so clean!" I was now squirming and scratching and unable to sit still.

I didn't know at the time but I know now: Lice doesn't care if hair is clean or dirty or if the home is clean or dirty. It doesn't matter if you're rich or poor . . . nope! There is no judgment by lice – they're an equal opportunity infestation.

How could this be? I swear I'd been doing the lice checks faithfully. I had seen no nits clinging to the shafts of her blonde hair. This was all happening pre-Internet so I couldn't even turn to Google for advice.

"Are you sure? How can you be so certain that it's lice?"

"Believe me when I tell you . . . it's lice and where there is one lousy louse, there's bound to be more. Do you know how many eggs one louse can . . ."

"STOP RIGHT THERE!" My legs were turning to Jello, spots were appearing in front of my eyes.

" . . . at least ten eggs a day and they can live up to thirty days. The eggs hatch in about seven to ten days, I believe . . ."

"I SAID STOP!" I needed to sit down and process this information. My little angel had waist-length hair that was potentially riddled with nits and maybe even more bugs!

At this point I could have easily roused both children from their warm beds and made them join us in a Silkwood shower with lice shampoo, but this was early 1990s and no pharmacy was open past six at night.

I tossed and turned all night. All I could think about was bugs crawling in my hair and in my bedding. Bugs clinging to every teddy bear in Amy's room, eggs sticking to jackets and toques.

I took the day off of work and spent the entirety of it treating my children with head lice shampoo and washing every sheet, pillowcase and quilt in the house. All of the stuffed animals were bagged and placed outside to freeze. I was never so pleased to see the temperature dip into the negative twenties and remain there throughout the day. I couldn't douse everything with gas and light it on fire, so I had to freeze the bugs to death.

The kids were curious but I managed to keep the secret from them. "This shampoo smells funny Mommy. Mommy, why are you scrubbing my head so hard? Mommy, why is my blankie outside in the cold?"

I finished sanitizing the house by bedtime and fell exhausted into my bed, the smell of bleach lingering on the sheets. My mind wouldn't stop racing. "What happens tomorrow when I send them back to that infested hellhole (aka/elementary school)? Everyone hangs their coats on the hooks by the door; no wonder lice can spread so quickly. It leaps from coat to coat and backpack to backpack. It's gonna happen again, I'm certain! Frankly, I don't think I can go through it again.

"Aha! What if I could figure out a way that my kids' jackets and backpacks don't have to co-mingle with the masses? What if . . . I sent them with a garment bag they can place their jackets, snowpants and backpacks inside before hanging them on the communal hooks?

"What if, when they returned home after school, they left their jackets and backpacks outside to freeze any unwanted creatures?

"What if, when they returned home from school, they changed out of their school clothes and into their play clothes and I washed their clothing every night?

"What if I braided Amy's hair so tightly that a wayward nit would need to be Houdini to work its way into her hairline?"

And so that's what I did.

My kids used a garment bag until they left elementary school and entered junior high, where they were given a personal locker. Amy never wore her hair free of braids until she turned thirteen. (Seriously. EVERY DAY . . . NO exceptions.)

And they never got infested again . . .

Breaking Point

• • •

It was 2001 and the anger had returned, and with it a sense of sadness that was a reminder of the paralyzing feeling I'd experienced after Amy was born.

I became a nasty, awful human being to my family and especially my husband. I was cruel and confused and anxious and unable to control my emotions. I was like a rubber band that was stretched to the breaking point.

And then it broke.

After returning from a vacation from hell, where I made it my mission to make everyone miserable, I made a doctor's appointment and then took a leave from work.

I was either depressed or I was a real bitch.

In this case it was clinical depression that turned me into a real bitch. I was sad, angry, unmotivated, felt worthless and was living a joyless existence. I was suffering another major depressive episode.

My days were spent getting the kids off to school and then I went back to bed for the day, sleeping on and off but more often just staring at the wall and suffering in silence.

I felt such hatred toward the world, but at the same time I wished someone could really see how badly I was feeling about feeling this way. I felt guilty that I was being a terrible mother, wife and daughter.

Recovery took longer this time. Medication was dispensed and then the dosage increased, with therapy back in the picture once again. Cognitive therapy was introduced which, it was hoped, would help me self-talk my way to happiness.

Cognitive therapy is designed to combat negative self-talk and the negative thinking that can manifest in a person's depressed brain. Personally, I can create a mountain out of any molehill and the therapy helped me combat those desperate, negative thoughts and the anxiety that was created as a result of those thoughts. For the first time, the doctors investigated the possibility that I was suffering from a bi-polar disorder. We tried lithium in conjunction with my other anti-depressants but there was no change. Thank goodness I wasn't manic depressive. Depression was one thing but being diagnosed with a bi-polar disorder was beyond my comprehension.

This was how my brain was working:

"What if the furnace quit working in the middle of the night when it's forty below and hubby isn't home? The house would freeze, the water pipes would burst and the water would flood the house, destroying everything. My plants would die, my electronics would be destroyed."

"What if I left the coffee pot on and it got really hot until it caught on fire?"

"What if I did the same with the iron?"

"What if I left the plug in the drain of the kitchen sink and the tap began to drip and the sink filled with water and then it ran all over the floor into the basement and . . ."

"If I do something wrong then I'm a terrible wife/mother."

"I'm a failure because I made a small mistake."

"They hate me because I'm not good enough."

"What if . . .?"

In my world, known as Judy's brain, it was always me who was responsible for everything. I am not going to be one of those people who blame their parent, but I will never forget seeing my mom standing at the window in our house in Worsley, silent tears streaming down her face, her shoulders heaving. It was after Dad's heart attack but before the big farm sale and move to Vancouver Island. She said to me, the 12-year-old me, "I don't know what I'm going to do". It was shocking to me to see her crumble like that, even if it was fleeting. This was my mom, a woman who never broke. Deep down I idolized that about her, although I now know that everyone breaks and that type of thinking is unhealthy. She didn't linger at the window long before she had dried her tears and continued to work like a superwoman getting our farm ready for the sale. That photo in my brain is never filed very far away.

Cognitive therapy was a lifesaver.

What if I left something on, or did something wrong? The cognitive therapy helped me to deter those automatic negative thoughts and, if they somehow got through my consciousness, then I learned to self-talk my way out of it.

"If the furnace quits working in the middle of the night when it's forty below and Bob isn't home I can call my Dad."

The sun will come up tomorrow.

Are You There, God? It's Me, Judy

• • •

I AM A CHRISTIAN . . . I think, although I haven't been baptized or chris-
tened or whatever Christians do to make it 'official'. In today's world, I
would categorize myself as a 'Facebook friend' of God – liking and sharing when someone posts some religious rhetoric that I can relate to, but
not fully committing by linking myself to a specific church. If being a
Christian was a Facebook event, I guess I waiver between 'I am attending' and 'Interested' – I'd have difficulty pressing the 'Not Attending'
button because I'd be concerned about a bolt of lightening.

How does one qualify as a Christian? I believe in God, but I haven't
made an effort to get to know Him very well. I could stumble my way
through a very light religious conversation, but if we begin referring to
passages in the Bible or in which version of the Bible the passage might
be found, I'd have to back away from the conversation. (FYI – when we
refer to which version that does not mean paperback, Kindle or e-book.)

As a child, my religious education focused primarily on sitting through studies with my grandmother and her fellow Jehovah's
Witnesses. She lived in a mother-in-law suite in our basement so it was
difficult to avoid. My father had grown up with his parents and most
of his siblings as members of the Jehovah's 'Witness church,[10]' but had
chosen not to join with them. In fact, Dad insisted that religion not play
any role in our upbringing, probably because of his confusing time as a
child.

---

10 Do they have churches? Is it called "attending church?"

49

This was weird for my mother, who was a practicing Anglican.[11] I know she would've loved to have us follow her religious upbringing, but Dad was insistent and said that we would be "allowed to make that decision as adults and not be forced into something as a child." Believe me, he carried an incredible weight of religious baggage.

I can see his point, but being part of a religion or receiving religious education is like learning to ride a bike. If you learn when you're eight years old, people forgive when you do silly things along the way. If you learn when you are twenty-five, the silly things you do or the silly questions you ask aren't quite as cute. If you're still struggling to understand at the age of fifty . . . is there any point anymore?

My dad *did* allow us to go to various churches with our friends to check them out and see what we thought. It was like blind dating a religion – we'd agree to meet in a public place and there were no strings attached. Stumbling to follow the up and down kneeling of the other parishioners or knowing that you're supposed to say, "Peace be with you" not "Pleased to meet you" was met with a giggle rather than a dirty look.

One of my favorite experiences was attending Bible Camp at our local United Church (which I refer to as religion-LITE). There were stories and crafts involving elbow macaroni. We sang and read books and I felt like all my past transgressions were being forgiven as I belted out the words to *The Old Rugged Cross*.

Excitedly I would return home and share my experience with my mom, who was the only one in the family who knew what I was talking about. In hindsight, my Jehovah's Witness grandmother would probably have enjoyed chatting about it, but somehow it didn't feel comfortable, especially when we were nearing the magical year of 1975.[12]

The 1970s, and 1975 in particular, was a critical timeline for my Jehovah's Witness extended family. Apparently, there was a very good

---

11 She is still Anglican of course, just not a practising Anglican. Best described as having a lifetime membership in something, but doesn't attend regular meetings – a member at large.
12 1975 was touted as quite possibly being the end of the world. Like an early Y2K without the computers.

chance that the world would end that year and for this eleven-year-old, the thought of the world ending was a tad terrifying. When would it happen? How would it happen? Would the sky be lit up with nuclear missiles? Would we be able to see the mushroom clouds from our house in Northern Canada? If my grandmother believes it, then it *must* be true . . . right?

My sister Jessie was profoundly affected by the prophecy and looming Armageddon – she was terrified and my parents did their best to dissuade her fears. Can you imagine? You're on the cusp of becoming a teenager and there is a possibility that you won't even be able to buy your first bra because the damn world's going to end! I also was aware of the conversations but for some reason I clung to the phrase, "no man knoweth[13]" that mom had taught me. Which meant, no one knows when IT will happen, not even Grandma. If I had to choose between believing my mom or my grandmother, I chose my mom. Mom wouldn't lie to me and if she believed that the world was coming to an end she'd certainly be preparing in some way....right?

We all know now that 1975 came and went with no brilliant red sunsets signifying that our world had ended, and those who'd believed the end was near were forced to focus their attentions elsewhere. Surely there was a plague to plan for somewhere.

Don't think in any way that I have a negative opinion about Jehovah's Witnesses. Everyone needs faith and my grandmother truly believed and wanted to share that faith with others. It just wasn't for me.

I continue to have blind dates with religion. I periodically will attend a church and I always leave feeling a bit sad that I have very little clue what they're referring to when they sing a hymn or read a passage.

I know my father was trying to protect us by allowing my sisters and I to make our own choices regarding religion, but in hindsight he agrees with me that we should have been able to accompany Mom to her church services and become baptized.

---

13 No man knoweth how to properly load dishwashers, either.

Now I guess I'm in limbo. Too old to attend Sunday School and too embarrassed to ask questions that someone going to Sunday School would already be able to answer.

And I repeated this same cycle with my own children . . .

Security Worry System Decoded

• • •

LAST YEAR BOTH MY CHILDREN traveled outside of North America. In advance of their trips, I came up with my own Security Worry System (SWS), somewhat designed like the Homeland Security Advisory System.

I replaced the traditional color-coded levels:

* Severe (red): severe risk
* High (orange): high risk
* Elevated (yellow): significant risk
* Guarded (blue): general risk
* Low (green): low risk

With the following:

Lotus (Anticipatory Worry): I will assume the lotus position and try to meditate myself to a worry-free state. This is the anticipatory worry level where one or both children are still on Canadian soil and all I can do is anticipate how worried I will become.

Pink: Slightly nauseated by worry. I will drink small amounts of Pepto Bismol when I am in this stage. This means that they are either (a) in the air or (b) cannot email, text or phone.

Benzodiazepine (common name, Ativan): Stressed by worry, can't be controlled by either yoga or Bepto Bismol. Requires anti-anxiety medication.

Tazer: Insane by worry to the point that I'm out of control. At this point may respond to a tazer.

The complete SWS system is available for a very low price. The kit contains the following:

- Yoga mat (you can choose from green or pink)
- Pepto Bismol (economy-size bottle)
- Benzodiazepine (5 x 2mg tablets)
- Purse-sized tazer (a liability waver must be signed prior to shipping)

All bundled up in a small, compact carrying case. It will conveniently fit in your purse! Your car! Your desk drawer! Call 1-800-SWS-CODE today!

Flew the Coop

• • •

THE KIDS HAVE BOTH LEFT home, leaving a vast wasteland of clean towels, turned-off lights, smaller water bills and tidy bedrooms. Sounds post-apocalyptic, doesn't it?

I thought I'd be prepared for it.

I had mocked those parents who spoke out about 'empty nest syndrome'. I mean, seriously, are you kidding me?

The day that I drove away leaving Amy at her college apartment I sobbed. For the months that followed I mourned the loss of her constant companionship. There were some days when I would leave wet towels on the bathroom floor just to have a connection with her because I knew, without a doubt that somewhere in her apartment was a pile of wet towels. Although my husband missed her just as much, he couldn't quite comprehend the depth of my despair.

Do you remember when you would smell your newborn baby's head? It was the most beautiful smell in the whole world. Well, I missed the smell of my firstborn baby's head.

Whew! Thank goodness Matthew still lived at home.

Until suddenly he didn't.

One day in a moment of frustration I said, "Matthew, maybe you should think about moving out one day." I had agonized about suggesting it but knew it might be time to throw the suggestion out there (all the parenting books recommended this approach).

That evening he came home after work, said he'd rented an apartment and stated that he could probably move out tomorrow.

WTF? Stop the bus! Hold the phone! I'd been bluffing!

When I suggested that he consider moving out, it was merely a suggestion. I was seed planting! You know, the same way I seed planted when I wanted one of the kids to break up with someone that I didn't quite approve of. I dropped little bits of information like, "I always figured you would go for someone with a sense of humor. Hmmmm . . . weird". The expeditious manner in which Matthew approached the whole moving out thing was terrifying. I mean . . . normally I had to ask him multiple times to do something: "Pick up your towel, pick up your towel, PICK UP YOUR TOWEL!"

Let the grieving begin . . . again.

With little more than his single bed, thirty-seven-inch television and fancy gaming console, he moved out the very next day.

As my husband so eloquently put it, "Way to go, Einstein! Now we're fucked."

The only way to salvage the situation was to invent Naked Tuesdays.

FYI? Don't come by on Tuesdays . . . I'm just sayin'.

4. Naked Tuesday

• • •

Naked Tuesday

• • •

. . . "AND THAT'S WHEN WE began celebrating Naked Tuesdays," I said, leaning back into the overstuffed couch pillows, taking a long, satisfying gulp of my vodka and iced tea. Phyllis's face had gone slack and she was staring at me. She was either having a stroke or she was totally caught off guard. I chose to believe the latter and said, "Phyllis . . . you should close your mouth . . . flies are getting in."

The shock visible in her voice, Phyllis managed to squeak out, "How marvelously naughty! How did you come up with such a genius idea?" Phyllis was clearly afternoon tipsy because she was using words like naughty and marvelously, but I knew that I'd truly surprised her with my confession.

Well, when the kids first moved out I found myself wandering aimlessly from room to room, feeling sorry for myself. I'd seriously begun to question my sanity. The toughest part? Only cooking for two people! I would lay out dinner (laying out dinner now meant taking the lids off the pots and dropping in mismatched serving spoons). The table was no longer used and had become a place to put our recycling, and hubby would look at the sheer volume of food and say, "Who'd you invite for dinner?" The dishwasher ran only once every three days and I noticed that there was dust in my oven. Yes, *dust* in my oven! The last bottle of ketchup had to be thrown out before we used it all because the best before date had expired, and the last peanut butter I purchased was one of those seniors-only-sized jars. You know . . . like a plastic baby food jar.

I remember the moment that it all changed . . .

I'd spent my first pajama-pant-clad Saturday watching a television marathon of *Say Yes to the Dress* and I realized, "I don't have to cook or clean or do laundry for anyone other than myself anymore. I can stay in bed all day. I can eat popcorn for dinner if I want. I can shower in the morning *and* have a bath at night. I can use all of the hot water! I'll always have a fresh towel available to me and I can finally buy expensive shampoo and have it all to myself!"

At first my husband was a little creeped out about my epiphany and the fact that we could live "like teenagers," but then he realized how freeing it was. It was about that point (two months into our newfound freedom) that I introduced the idea of Naked Tuesdays.

"Naked Tuesdays?" he said with a puzzled expression on his face. "Why Tuesday? And why on earth would we want to be naked?"

"It doesn't have to be Tuesday," I responded. "But I like the idea of it being the same day each week. It's easier to plan for it . . . you know what I mean . . . when we're making appointments and stuff." It was painfully clear that even while living like teenagers I couldn't commit one hundred per cent to a world without structure or schedule.

"What if someone comes over?" he said, struggling with my reasoning.

"We tell everyone that Tuesday is hereby known as Naked Tuesday: Please don't come over on Tuesday or it'll be weird." I smiled then, because I was imagining the look on someone's face if I were to actually say that.

"Look honey (I'd found that using terms like 'honey' and 'sweetie' were critical to gaining the upper hand in a conversation), the kids are grown and have moved out. We have no grandchildren and the dogs don't care what we look like as long as we feed them. I don't know what the big deal is. I've been working up to this for a couple of weeks now. Haven't you noticed that I now go bra-free on Sundays?"

With that comment, Bob flushed like a teenager and smiled. "Yes, I noticed and I *was* going to say something, but then I figured you were just expressing yourself after finishing that *Going Grey at Fifty* book." Immediately his face transformed, the naughty smile now gone and a worried expression complete with deeply furrowed brows appeared. "Or maybe you forgot? You didn't simply forget to put a bra on, did you?" he whispered, holding his breath, terrified of my possible response. My grandmother had suffered with Alzheimer's disease and I'm sure he was thinking that first it would be the bra, then I'd forget the pants and then I'd go to Safeway without either. We were still recovering from the dog-ate-the-back-out-of-my-pants-but-I-didn't-notice-and-went-downtown-shopping-anyway debacle.

"No, I didn't forget. And FYI? The book was *Fifty Shades of Grey.* No, I was celebrating the fact that there's no one here but us chickens! No one cares if I wear a bra or not. There are no teenagers here that I have to worry about seeing my untethered bosom. Frankly, I love the freedom and so do the girls," I said, pointing to my chest.

"Isn't it a bit . . . unsanitary?" he asked, clearly beginning to flesh out the idea of going naked in his brain.

"It simply takes some preparation. Throw sheets onto the couch and living room chair and, if you must work on the computer, use the leather chair. For God's sake, don't accidently turn the web cam on! Coffee would have to be sipped very carefully and perhaps a dish towel should cover your lap when you're eating. The ten-second rule doesn't apply on Naked Tuesday. Other than that, it should be no different than any other day."

"What about our meals? I guess I wouldn't expect bacon and eggs on Naked Tuesday." Bob chuckled to himself, knowing that he'd made a 'funny'. Funny because I *never* cook breakfast and of course funny because . . . well I'm sure you know why.

I could've chosen to be offended by that last remark but I didn't want to interrupt the flow of the negotiation, which seemed to be headed for an agreement without a lot of compromise (pigs were clearly flying). "We'd definitely need to plan our meals, and we can agree that I won't be frying any bacon, but that doesn't mean we'll suffer. Oven baking or using the microwave can result in pretty decent food. Also, it's *only* one day, and it isn't like either of us can't go *one* day with a little less food."

I could see Bob was intrigued with the idea. He was imagining enjoying Naked Tuesday with no expectations. Obviously no yard work was anticipated and he wouldn't be expected to run any errands downtown. In winter he could languish on the sheet-clad couch and watch the snowflakes gather, knowing there'd be no requirement to shovel. In summer, he could do the same: sit back and watch the grass grow while sipping on a cold beer. "So . . . basically I could spend the day like you always do . . . but I'll be naked?" With that comment Bob started to laugh so hard he began coughing and let out a wee 'toot' and then, of course, he laughed harder.

He sputtered the following while laughing at his flatulence like a fourteen-year-old boy: "Now that'd be funny! What if I 'sharted' on Naked Tuesday! Did you think about that, Einstein?" Tears were now running down Bob's face.

I'm not an idiot. After thirty-plus years of marriage, I had indeed thought about that particular phenomenon and felt I'd completed a risk assessment of the possibility of that situation. "We would be super careful about what we eat on Mondays. For example, you wouldn't be able to have any onions on Monday and, of course, no Indian food."

"What about you, my little Farty McPrincess?" asked Bob. "You'll have to swear off cheese completely."

"I can do that. I know I can." I wanted Naked Tuesday to happen more than I'd wanted anything for a long time and would do whatever it took to make it successful.

At this point Bob got up and gave me a hug. "If you really want this I'm here for you, sweetheart." And then he began to laugh again because he knew that the hug was being accompanied by another 'toot' and believe me . . . it smelled as if something had died.

While I'd been telling my story, Phyllis had poured us each another vodka and iced tea, with more vodka than iced tea. I was concerned she wouldn't be able to make her way home down the back alley access.

"I love you," slurred Phyllis. "You're my hero. I want Naked Tuesdays, too!"

I knew this would happen. I knew that if I told folks about Naked Tuesday they'd want to participate. I shook my head. "*We* have Tuesdays, Phyllis. You can't have Tuesdays."

Oh my! Phyllis looked crestfallen. It was as if I'd told her there was no more vodka! "You can have Wednesdays, sweetie, or even Thursdays. I don't recommend Mondays or Fridays." I gave her a congratulatory hug.

Raising my glass, I reached forward to make a toast. "To Naked Tuesday!" I yelled, the last of my drink swishing over the edge of the glass and spilling all over Phyllis, who was now ugly-girl-drunk and crying, "To Naked Wednesdays!"

Out of the Mouth of Bob's

● ● ●

THE OTHER DAY BOB AND I were going somewhere and we had to stop at the ATM to pick up some cash. As I grabbed the 'holy crap' handle[14] to haul my five-foot-one-inch frame back into the lifted pickup, my husband turned to me and said (with a sigh people, *with a sigh!*), "I guess I've changed, too" and then he returned his gaze to the road and proceeded to back out of the parking space.

Shocked and a bit out of breath, considering I had just lifted my own body weight, I said, "What the heck does that mean . . . you guess you've changed too?"

Now I was upset. "Why would you say something like that to me? Of course I've changed. We both have changed! You don't hear me saying anything about your thinning hair or your expanding waste line. Why would you say something like that to me? Do you know how that makes me feel?"[15]

As we now drove in silence (oh yeah, you could hear a pin drop) I proceeded to text my daughter with the details of her father's transgression and then I called Sister #1. I then did what every social media savvy woman does in the twenty-first century: I posted his comment on my Facebook timeline for all my friends to see.

It happened again. You'd think he'd learn . . .

---

14 Fat-ass lift assist handle located on the inside of a heavy-duty pickup.

15 What I really wanted to say was, "I don't pay you to think!" But considering he entered into this marriage contract willingly, it didn't really fit.

Recently, I acquiesced and rode along with hubby as he had to go back to work to tend to something "mechanicky". I thought to myself, "Hey! This might qualify as *couple time* when I report back to my life coach."

You see . . . I never, ever go with him. He asks, oh he asks quite often actually, but you know, *Grey's Anatomy* isn't going to watch itself.

Another reason I don't participate in a ride-along is because at some point he begins speaking 'Gas Operator' to me and frankly, my piece of measuring string is not calibrated to deal with KPI and flow and . . . you know. I listen but I don't compute.

The evening was uneventful. We spent twenty minutes driving out to the site, twenty minutes doing whatever needed to be done, ten minutes monitoring and then we headed for home.

I brought three books, a full bottle of water, my fully charged iPad and a bag of snacks – clearly I was over-prepared for the adventure. I stopped short of bringing my ear buds because . . . well, that might be construed as being rude.

It was a beautiful spring evening. The skies were a light blue and the fresh green was just beginning to appear on the trees. The sun was beginning to dip on the horizon and there was this glittery glow on the grass and tree line. The pollen and fluff in the air was clearly visible, just floating along, and the weird pre-dusk light made it strangely beautiful.

Supertramp[16] began to play on the radio and I began to hum along. Out of the corner of my eye I saw hubby's arm reach slowly out towards me, fingers curled softly as if to caress my cheek. Thirty-plus years of marriage and he still has the ability to melt my heart.

Smiling, I turned my head to him as if to say with my eyes, "Sweetheart, I'm so glad I came with you."

"Turn your head back a little into the light," he whispered. "I can see a big hair on your chin. I can get it for you!"

---

16 Supertramp brings back memories of sitting in the back of my friend's trailer drinking Southern Comfort and coke.

I Guess I've Changed, Too

● ● ●

I SPENT THE FOLLOWING DAYS vacillating between feeling hurt by my hubby's comment and realizing that perhaps I've now become the 'after' picture in my own reality series. You know, the picture of that woman with poor skin, wrinkles on her face, a few (okay, forty) extra pounds. What the hell happened to me?

It is not like I haven't been trying . . .

Years ago, in my thirty-ninth year of life, and after careful consideration,[17] I decided I'd take the plunge and get my eyes done. No, not Lasik surgery; something a little more vain. I wanted to get my eyelids done – 'blepharoplasty' – which involves the removal of the excess skin from the upper lid. Why would this be an issue at the young(ish) age of thirty-nine? Were they obscuring my vision? No, I just hated that I had droopy eyes and wanted to do it before I turned forty. Everyone always said I had bedroom eyes. For years I thought they meant I had sexy eyes, but now I realize they just felt that I looked tired. Basically, my bedroom eyes had fallen and could no longer get up.

So, after investigating great plastic surgeons, I decided that I'd travel to the big city for the procedure. Jessie accompanied me.

I opted to remain awake for the 'procedure' for a couple of reasons: (1) It was less expensive, and (2) It was considerably less expensive. The

17 aka: Endless Google searching.

66

doctor had prescribed Ativan for me to take a half-hour prior to the procedure. They recommended one, so I took two.[18]

Thoroughly drugged and a little giggly, I sat in the waiting room looking through the before and after booklets, secretly wondering if any of the gauze-wrapped, oversized-black-sunglasses-adorned ladies around me were frequent fliers and might be in the book already. Everyone spoke very quietly, in breathless whispers. In retrospect, I now know that they were whispering because they couldn't move their mouths due to the swelling. But at the time it was all very glamorous.

An extremely large-breasted woman with eyebrows in her hairline called me into the procedure room. Her face hardly moved . . . clearly someone who was abusing the fact that one of the perks of her employment was free procedures. We'll call her 'Joan'.

I reclined on what resembled a dental/gyno/massage chair and tried to relax, not realizing I had a death grip on some pamphlets I'd been reading in the waiting room. Joan draped my face with sterile towels, leaving only my eyes visible to the doc. Was I freaking? Nah. What could go wrong?

In walked the doc. He was a very fit and attractive man, but only about five feet tall. In my Ativan-induced giggly state I immediately tagged him 'Tiny' (as in Tiny Tim). Joan positioned a small, turquoise Rubbermaid stool beside the chair for Tiny to use and the surgery began. Oh . . . did I mention that his little surgical slippers were super cute and his green scrubs were hemmed with little cuffs? I wanted to squeeze his cheeks. Clearly, two Ativan are more than I can handle, as I was hallucinating that a Leprechaun was performing the procedure.

First came the freezing. His tiny, teeny fingers wielded a tiny needle injecting a substance into my eyelids. I recall being able to still open them, but I couldn't feel them. Once this was confirmed with a gentle poke of my eyelid and the question "Can you feel this?"[19] His small,

---

18 Don't try this at home.

19 Spoken with the high voice of the little men that sang, "Follow the yellow brick road, follow the yellow brick road."

gloved, childlike hands began working their magic, the scalpel cutting a small crescent out of the right eyelid, then the left. In horror, I realized that I could now see out of the narrow slits he'd created! At that point I may have passed out . . .

"Blink, Judy!" said Joan, her impressive breasts only inches from my face.

I tentatively[20] blinked. Satisfied with his handiwork, the doctor then sewed up my now taut, wrinkle-free lids and placed an ice-filled sleeping mask over my new and improved eyes.

Giddy with the realization that I would no longer look like Wilfred Brimley, I blurted, "Do you have time to do my lips while I'm here? I want this!" And I unfolded the pamphlets I'd been clutching in my sweaty hands.

What I wanted done was a Restylane[21] injection into my lips. I have thin lips and I soooooo wanted a pouty mouth (I already had a potty mouth). Once my Visa card was scanned and approved, they came back in with a syringe and a vial of clear liquid. "Now, this may be a bit pain-ful, Judy, but it will be over quickly" and Tiny Tim began to inject liquid filler into my lips with what I can only assume (because it hurt so very much) was a NUMBER TWO PENCIL![22] Just when I thought I couldn't take it any more and was really regretting my decision, he announced that he was finished.

Staggering, I was handed off to Jessie for safekeeping and her watch-ful eye. "What the hell happened to you?" she asked, looking horrified.

"I goth my lipth dun, too . . . aren't I piddy?"

Two weeks later . . .

My eyes are fantastic! Although they didn't close completely for the first little while (freaked my husband out when I slept), they looked

---

20 I think I needed to blink to ensure that there was still sufficient eyelid remaining to close my eyes.

21 An injectable that lasts 3-6 months. The more you move the injected area, the faster it dissolves . . . mine would probably only last a month.

22 Actually, it was a very small needle but it felt like a pencil.

amazing. I looked younger and refreshed. I felt so Hollywood; I even purchased large, oversized dark sunglasses for the flight back.

My lips . . . well, that was a horrifying experience and I hadn't told my husband I'd got them done prior to arriving home. It was to be a surprise. If the look on the Westjet flight attendant's face was any indication, it was going to be a *big* surprise.

Put Some Butter on It

• • •

SINCE GIVING UP RUNNING, I'VE taken a water jogging class. I loved the class. Very low impact but quite a workout. A piece of cake, right? Wrong! I had plenty of trouble in the change room. Like many women, I'm self-conscious about getting undressed in front of other people.

This is what happened.

After an energetic water jogging class I rushed downstairs so I could get a change cubicle with a curtain. I was anxious about someone inadvertently pulling the curtain open while I was changing, so I quickly whipped off my suit and started to get dressed, neglecting to dry off properly.

Wrapping the towel around my waist, I grabbed my jog bra and proceeded to pull it over my head. WRONG. It got stuck. I was still wet and the jog bra was made out of Lycra fabric. I was now standing half-naked with a jog bra stuck at my elbows covering my face. I tried to work it down but nothing would help. At that point the towel that was loosely wrapped around my waist fell to my feet. I began to weep softly, the stretchy, soft fabric absorbing my tears. I had no choice but to ask for help.

Bending at the waist like a diver and using my tightly bound arms, I gently pulled the curtain aside slightly to see who might be in the change room. There was a young girl, about thirteen years old, combing out her wet hair. I knew this was going to be a life-changing moment for her, a moment she would never, ever forget. Taking a deep breath, I quietly asked for help. "Just focus on my unshaven armpits and tug . . . "

2007 and a Series of Unfortunate Events

● ● ●

AT THE BEGINNING OF 2007 I resolved to become a 'Beacon of Light' and shine the light of happiness upon all those around me.

It didn't happen.

Bob and I traveled to Mexico that February, Cabo San Lucas to be specific, for some sun, sand and big drinks with little umbrellas. As we de-planed in Cabo and entered the luggage area, we were surrounded by 'greeters' (defined as smiling locals promising us free trips if we went to a timeshare presentation). I encouraged Hubby to get rid of them and, moments later, he had us booked on a timeshare presentation for the next morning. "But Jude,[23] we get a free glass-bottom boat tour and tickets for the Pirate Ship Excursion![24] Oh . . . and not one but *two* bottles of their finest Tequila."

When we checked into our all-inclusive hotel, looking forward to our oceanfront view and king-sized bed (we'd booked six months earlier, specifically requesting it), we were disappointed. The room we were now booked into was located one kilometre from the lobby and faced into a wall of sand. Recalling my resolution to be the Beacon of Light, I offered[25] to deal with the situation.

---

23 Very few folks are allowed to call me Jude. My mother and my husband are two of those VIPs.

24 Remind me to tell you what happened on the Pirate Ship Excursion.

25 I insisted, because Bob had questionable negotiation skills – he was a pushover.

Juan and I had a long conversation – no voices were raised – and we were moved to a better location. We did, indeed, have waterfront (there was a pool close by) and the melodic voices of the underpaid[26] laborers constructing the new wing of the hotel were almost music to our ears, beginning at six each morning.

The next morning we rose bright and early to be available for the shuttle transporting us to our timeshare presentation. Jill, an expatriate from Canada, promised us a low-pressure tour of the high-rise condominium. Unfortunately, low-pressure Jill quickly became an embittered, childless, thirty-something shrew and, when we refused to buy in, she sent us on our way sans transportation; we hiked two kilometres on the beach back to our hotel. But, never fear, we had two teeny, tiny bottles of shitty, poor-quality tequila and a voucher for a Pirate Ship Ride in our sweaty hands.

The shopping in Cabo can be fun, and walking the inner harbor is one of the attractions. Our hotel was quite a distance from the downtown core and one of the 'quaint' touristy ways of getting to the downtown is riding the water taxi. Now, the water was extremely rough in front of our hotel, going from sandy beach to very deep – in a short distance. The water taxis didn't come into a dock; they came in on a saltwater wave up onto the sand and you leaped onto the boat. It was all very 'exciting'. Having used the water taxi twice already, I fancied myself as a bit of an expert.

When you disembarked from the taxi in the inner harbor, you climbed conveniently out onto a dock.

The return to the hotel isn't quite as easy and timing is critical – specifically, the moment when you should jump from the boat onto the sandy beach. Do you know how to say in Spanish, "Hey lady, I think it is safe to jump onto the beach now?" No? Well, I don't either but that's what I thought he said as we were coming in on a rogue wave and I leaped, yes I leaped, INTO 15 FEET OF SALT WATER, completely dressed, with purse, *all* of our traveller's checks and all our cash. Hubby, sweet man

---

26 I have no clue if they were underpaid or not. It just made the story sound better.

that he is, forgot that I was a former competitive swimmer[27] and jumped in after me, new digital camera and all . . .

In the moments that I was underwater I had an opportunity to reflect on my life and what was important. As I broke the surface I verbalized this by turning and swearing at the water taxi driver. He was unconcerned and already maneuvering his boat into open water. There were plenty more tourists where we came from.

I know from the movies that in these situations the lady will emerge from the water like a nymph moving out of the waves, but you don't. I didn't know weather to laugh (along with those on the beach) or cry. For the record . . . I *did* stick the landing.

---

27 One race when I was twelve. But it still counts because I received a participant ribbon.

Sometimes When We Touch

• • •

SINCE BOB TURNED FIFTY HE has become very reflective on his life, his goals, and about eventual retirement.

Myself, I don't think about that stuff. There is simply not enough antidepressant medication to help me down that road. I don't want to think about the near misses, the what ifs, and I don't like to imagine my life without him.

Bob wants to live 'off the grid' out in the wilderness, not relying on anything or anyone. Basically, he wants to kill the bacon and then he wants me to cook it.

The silver lining? Being that far away from civilization, the authorities would have a difficult time finding the body . . . his body. We wouldn't last a month.

Why?

We'd have to talk – to each other, *only* each other. In our thirty-plus years of marriage we've said everything there is to say to each other. Now we'd begin that stage of our lives known as the 'repeats', aka: repeats of previous conversations. Basically we were going into syndication but instead of the *Love Boat*[28], it could end up being *Dexter.*[29]

I also couldn't handle the constant attention, and by 'attention' I mean guidance and by 'guidance' I mean him correcting me all the time.

---

28 Someone falls in love in every episode.
29 Someone dies in every episode.

A few years ago he took a two-month sabbatical from work. He needed to relax and unwind. Don't get me wrong, it was well deserved.

By the way . . . I chose to begin writing this while he was relaxing at home.[30] Co-inky dink? I think not.

These are the moments when you wish you had a sister-wife.

During his time relaxing he did tend to provide me with guidance . . . often. In fact, he provided me with so much guidance that I began to question how on earth I'd managed thus far.

I had no clue as to the number of daily activities requiring a slight correction or modification. I'm simply thankful that we had this time together. Implementing these 'corrections' would no doubt make me a better wife, homemaker and mother.

For example, for some stereotypical reason, meal preparation has always been my thing and I have unwillingly embraced this role throughout my marriage. I would prepare a meal and he would always be impressed with the outcome, no matter how sad and pathetic the effort was (soup and sandwiches, scrambled eggs, etc.).

During his sabbatical he had the chance to go 'behind the scenes' of the operation and see what all the fuss was about. More importantly, he could provide instruction on how to improve on said operation.

I know he was expecting Cirque De Soleil but instead he was greeted with Barnum and Bailey. There were no death-defying leaps; there was simply the occasional spider monkey juggling act.

I was busted.

There was no sword-swallowing or flame-juggling and only sporadic knife-throwing. There was no floor show. The only excitement was when I dropped a plate.

Since that time of forced togetherness, things have changed. Now when I produce a bowl of soup and a sandwich, I don't get the same enthusiastic response. I have found that I've grown weary of cooking.

---

30 Underfoot.

Recently I overheard two women discussing what they were making for dinner and I remarked (wanting to get into the conversation), "Ugh . . . I am *so sick* of making meals."

I expected empathy and understanding and instead I got a sad nod and, "When I'm your age I might feel that way, too."

Food Fight

• • •

THE FOLLOWING IS A TRANSCRIPT of a conversation between a couple trying to make dinner plans. It may or may not be based on real events – you decide.

"Let's go out for dinner."

"Okay . . . where do you want to go?"

"You decide!"

"No . . . I picked last time. You decide"

"You didn't pick last time, I did! Remember? We had an argument over whether or not they served Palace Chicken at (namewithheld) and you said they didn't, but I was certain they served a variation of it and I was right."

"Oh . . . yeah. I guess you did pick last time. Go ahead and pick again if you want."

"You just want me to choose so if it turns out crappy you can blame me! YOU CHOOSE!"

"Okay, fine! Let's go to the same place again."

"Oh sure, taking the easy way out. I don't want to go back there again, I want something different."

"Okay, what about getting a burger somewhere?"

"I'm not opposed to getting a burger. Are you thinking fast food or sit-down?"

"Sit-down."

"Okay, where?"

"What about . . . Fancyburgersitdownrestaurant?"

"Ummmmmm . . . remember how dark it is in there? And they turn the music up really loud after seven o'clock and it's already six forty-five."

"Okay. Well then, what about Notasfancysitdownrestaurant?"

"Yeah, that's an option but it's going to be really busy tonight because of the concert."

"Well then let's just do fast food burgers – quick and easy."

"Ughhhh. I had McFastFood for lunch. I can't do fast food twice in one day."

"Did you do drive-thru or walk-in? If you did drive-thru no one will recognize you if we walk in this time."

"That isn't the point. The point is that unless you're Morgan Spurlock[31] filming a documentary about poor eating habits, no one should eat fast food twice in one day."

"You're eating in restaurants TWICE in one day. Aren't you splitting hairs here?"

"Oh gawd! Don't say *hair*! Remember when I found that big hair in my salad?"

(Both suffer gag reflex.)

"Why don't we go to Nottoohotnottoospicy?"

"How many times do I have to tell you, I love Indian food but Indian food doesn't love me! I can't do the spicy curry."

"You know, just once I'd like to eat something a wee bit interesting instead of pizza and burgers. I never get to go to Nottoohotnottoospicy!"

"Hey, don't let me stop you. I can just as easily stay home and have a bowl of soup."

"I'm not going out for dinner all by myself!"

"Well then, we're going to have to come to some type of decision. It's already seven o'clock and you know how weird my dreams get if I eat too late in the evening."

"Fine. Let's just go to Burgerwithacrown and do take-out. Will you go and pick it up?"

---

31 American documentary filmmaker of Academy Award Nominated docudrama *"Super Size Me."*

"They're renovating Burgerwithacrown – remember?"

"Crap! You're right. Well then, should we just order pizza?"

"Pizza sounds good."

"Sure . . . But it has to be gluten-free, remember?"

"Ugghhh. Can't you eat gluten just this once? Just to make it easier?"

"No, I CAN'T EAT GLUTEN JUST THIS ONCE! My body is really sensitive and I'll be sick all evening!"

"Funny . . . you didn't seem to be as married to your Gluten-Free Diet the other evening when you polished off a sleeve of crackers with butter!"

(Insert snorting laughter here.)

"Were you spying on me?!"

"No, I didn't need to spy on you to figure that one out. There was a butter knife in the sink and an empty cracker sleeve in the garbage. Plus there were even crumbs in your hair."

(Folds in half, laughing hysterically.)

"Forget dinner. I'm not hungry anymore!"

"Oh don't be pissy like that! I'm just bugging you sweetheart! I'll go get your gluten-free pizza and we can watch a movie together. You pick the movie!"

(Big lopsided smile, feeling remorseful about making light of food sensitivity – moves in for a hug.)

"No, I picked last time. You decide."

When Hubby Leaves the Nest . . . Alone

● ● ●

So MY HUSBAND JUST CALLED me to tell me about some excitement at work . . .

The phone rang and I immediately recognized the crackle on the phone line as his phone synced with his hands-free device.

He only works about twenty miles from town, but strangely, it always seems like we're having one of those CNN satellite interviews with a two- or three-second delay.

"Good morning!" I answered cheerfully because, well, he was at work and I was at home drinking my coffee and enjoying my day and I wanted to sound grateful.

"Judy, you'll never believe what just happened!" he said breathlessly.

Worried enough to put my coffee cup down and switch the phone to the other hand, I said quietly, carefully enunciating each and every word, "What! What just happened?"

After thirty-one years of marriage I still can't pin down when something is an emergency or not. I mean, he can calmly call me and say, "Hey, you'll never guess what just happened" and it could turn out to be that he just stabbed himself in the upper thigh with a filleting knife and was now driving himself from his ice fishing location into the hospital whilst compressing the wound with a diaper he found in the truck.

"Hey, you'll never guess what just happened?" is also a phrase used for happy things like, "I just rescued a baby deer that was stuck in the ditch."

So forgive me if I prepared myself for the worst-case scenario.

"You remember yesterday when I told you that I'd poked that hornet's nest outside the door of the building?"

I nodded in response on my end of the phone. Whether or not I had actually listened to him yesterday and paid any attention to what he was saying was irrelevant at this point.

He must have realized that fact as well, because he didn't wait for an acknowledgement, he just continued talking. "Well today I knew I was going to have to deal with the nest because it can't be left there . . . someone's going to get stung. The hornets out there aren't hornets like when we were kids; *these* white-faced hornets are angry buggers and easily pissed off. They act like you do when you suddenly have no wi-fi. Hahahahahaha!"

Yeah . . . you're funny, Bob.

Chuckling to himself at the funny he just made, he continued. "So I park the truck a ways away and I leave the door open in case I need to have an escape plan. I look for my long stick that I used yesterday but for some reason I can't find it anywhere. Crap! Like Tom Cruise in *Top Gun* I realize that *It's too close for missiles, I'm switching to guns* and I have to go to Plan B, which is: a shorter stick. I reach behind the seat to look for my snowbrush that I *know* is there because, have I told you I'm like the last Boy Scout? I'm always prepared. I'm so prepared I have a snowbrush in my pickup twelve months of the year. Anyway . . . I find my snowbrush and begin psyching myself up for the crash and dash. Coveralls have been zipped and snapped up to my chin. Hardhat is in place. Shoelaces on boots have been knotted and then knotted again. Gloves are on. Safety glasses are on. I'm goin' in."

Realizing that this S*tory Time with Bob* is going to take a while, I put the phone down and placed it on speaker so I could continue drinking my coffee.

"Wow! What happened next?" I said, hoping to match my excitement to his level of excitement and relaxing a little because the story wouldn't be taking as long if there were any arterial bleeds.

"Well . . . like I said, I leave the door of the truck open in case I need to escape and I creep up to that hornets' nest and I can hear them.

They're mighty pissed off at something, which is ridiculous because it was a beautiful day and that proves they're crazy because there's nothing to make them angry. Yet."

At this point the phone crackled and got all staticky (new word I just made up) and he paused his story until it cleared again.

"So I get close enough to the nest and realize how short the damn snowbrush really is and figure that I basically need to be directly underneath the nest in order to knock it down. I look at the truck and judge the terrain (level but lumpy with gravel) and distance (thirty feet) and hope like hell I can make it to safety unscathed and unstung. At this point, every muscle is tense, like an Olympic runner, and I'm prepared to Usain Bolt my way to the truck."

I was completely engrossed in his story. Would the hornets survive? Would Bob survive? Would he make it to safety in time? Why does he get himself in these situations? I was at the edge of my seat and wished I had popcorn.

Sensing that he had me completely engaged, he decided to go all in. "I suddenly decide to go for it and I hit the nest whilst simultaneously pivoting and springing forward to launch me back towards the truck, hoping to outrun the angry hornets. But just then . . . SNAP! SNAP! The sound is like a gun shot and I immediately find myself on the ground writhing in pain."

"Oh my goodness! Were you stung? What happened?" My mind raced with possibilities.

"Well, Judy, the unthinkable happened. I pulled not one, but two, muscles in my leg and down I went. It must have been because I was so tense and, in hindsight, I probably should've done some stretching. Frantically, I begin dragging myself towards the truck because I'm certain that the hornets are a heartbeat away from attacking me."

Pipe in the song *The End* by The Doors (from *Apocalypse Now*).

A weird noise interrupted the conversation and I was a bit irritated until I understood that it was the sound of me snorting with laughter. Thankfully I'd placed him on speakerphone because it allowed me to cover my face to attempt to disguise the noise. I don't want him to think that I don't care . . .

"When I was about twenty feet away I managed to get to my feet and limp to the truck. My right leg was stiff in spasm and I walked like I'd just filled an adult diaper."

"What about the hornets? Did you get stung?"

"Pfft! The hornets ignored me completely! It was as if they knew there was more chance I'd hurt myself than hurt them. This being over fifty sucks. You know that? If I was ten years younger . . . well . . . it would have been different."

I couldn't contain the laughter and I began to whoop and snort at the same time, which elicited sharp flatulence that scared the dog.

"Oh.My.Gawd. You are sooooooo funny." I was completely relaxed now because I knew nothing horrible had happened, that my stiff-legged hubby would return to me this day.

"Yeah, it was funny wasn't it?" And Bob chuckled with me, knowing that the story was pretty darn funny. "Do we have any of that muscle-rub stuff? It really does hurt."

"Of course we do, sweetheart . . . of course we do."

5. Snap, Crackle and Pop!

• • •

Cereal Murder

● ● ●

I WALKED ACROSS THE KITCHEN floor the other day and heard a loud popping noise.

Insert sad emoticon here.

I didn't want any more children, but the realization that my eggs were now exploding inside myself saddened me. I wondered if they were all going to go at once or if it was going to happen over a period of time. Was it going to be days, weeks or months? I could imagine them ducking and running for cover with sniper shots coming at them, envisioning herring caught in a net, flapping to get away, gasping for air. Spontaneous combustion . . . poof!

My eggs are no longer agile twenty-something's; this will not be a fair fight.

They've been together in that tiny space for over fifty years now, like little soldiers waiting to be called up one by one. Science states that at one point there were approximately seven million of them, then six hundred thousand, then at puberty, finally settling in at about four hundred thousand . . . all in one teeny, tiny space. Can you imagine?

Who decides who's called up each month? Did they throw a goodbye party? What do they say to the lucky ones? Perhaps, "Grab your things, you're getting out today."

I compare it to those misfits in the movie *Armageddon* when Bruce Willis offers to try and blast the asteroid heading for earth. They're going in a blaze of glory but they have no guarantee they'll survive. They may simply be taking one for the team, doing it for their country. Not to imply that my unused ovum are a collection of misfits, although I'm sure there are some duds (future Kardashians) in the bunch. All of this happens as Aerosmith sings, "I don't want to miss a thing."

But I digress. Right now I was mourning the loss of three hundred thousand of my closest friends and I was trying to remember how many stages of grief I needed to go through. Five? Seven? Denial, anger, bargaining, depression and acceptance . . . was I already at acceptance?

I was letting them go so easily. Like the scene from *Titanic* when the boat was going down and the elderly couple climbed into their bed and waited for the water to rise. It was my time.

"Goodbye old friends."

Taking another step I hear another pop. Looking heavenward, shaking my fists, I cry, "Are you kidding me? Give them a chance!"

Then I realized.

I'd stepped on a Rice Krispie.

Milk, Bread, Eggs . . .

● ● ●

AND ON TOP OF IT all, you begin to lose your fucking memory.

Those little, teeny, tiny ovum exploding like Rice Krispies have packed their going-away case filled with bits and pieces of my brain.

They don't take the unnecessary shit, like the answer to the question, "If Train 'A' was leaving the station at eight o'clock, traveling east at seventy miles per hour . . . ," they take the important stuff like, "Where did I leave my cell phone?"

I've become the lady in the commercial who has to record her grocery list into a digital recorder that she clips to her purse. Next thing you know I'll be purchasing an inordinate number of lemons, or milk, or cans of tomato soup or whatever, and they'll be stashed in strange places like under the sink or the microwave.

This is why you see older women packing their purses everywhere they go. It isn't because they don't trust anyone. It's because they're afraid they'll forget where they put it.

The Last Password Standing

• • •

"PLEASE CHOOSE A NEW PASSWORD." As my eyes skimmed the five words I felt sickened, almost light-headed, with the realization that today might just become *that* day . . . the day I'd known would come eventually, but that I'd feared with an unhealthy fear. Today would become the day that I ended up using 'the last password'.

How did this happen? How did we get here . . . now . . . today?

We're all born with a certain number of things; the obvious are arms, legs, fingers, toes, brain cells, ovum, etc. But I also believe the human body contains a limited supply of computer passwords. Yes, that's correct. It's a little known fact that we are born with a limited supply of these word/number/uppercase/lowercase combinations and that when you run out, you're shit out of luck. Sure, you can go back and begin re-using something you used in the late 1990s, but honestly, they say you're sacrificing your online security.

A good password is like an old friend. It rolls off your fingers onto the computer keyboard with nary a backward glance. A bad password makes you stumble; trips you up. We all do the unacceptable with our password selection. A good password with good 'security strength' contains a magical combination of uppercase and lowercase letters with a few numbers thrown in for good measure. It shouldn't be your wedding anniversary date with the initials of your children added. It shouldn't be the name of your first boyfriend/girlfriend. It's supposed to be completely random and hard to remember, because if it's hard for *you* to remember, then it certainly should be difficult for a hacker to hack.

My point is, we've all had good passwords and bad passwords in our lives. A good password is comforting, like a warm blanket; a bad password irritates you every time you use it.

Which brings me to now, today, the day that I might have to break out my last good password. Why is it my last? I honestly don't think I have another really great one in me. I always thought that I would be in my sixties or even seventies before I used my last really good password. But between online banking, Skype, Twitter, LinkedIn, iTunes, Facebook, Instagram, Pinterest, Snapchat and now Google+, I've used up my passwords like the world has squandered its opportunities to fight climate change. Now it's time to pay the piper.

I really should have buried a list of passwords in the backyard, simply because I knew a day like this would arrive, a day where there was no way my aging brain would be able to come up with a password that was going to be acceptable and meet all of the *uppercase, lowercase, contain a capitalization and a number* criteria. I would have secured it much in the same way as the Cold War launch sequence codes, the Cadbury Secret or the KFC magical combination of herbs and spices: I would have hidden the perfect password in a coffee tin and buried it in the backyard.

Today, instead of sitting here frustrated about having to come up with a new combination of letters and numbers, I would be outside digging in the backyard. I can imagine that as I began to dig one hole, then two, then three, I'd realize that I should have told someone where I'd buried my hidden treasure.

Cold, and with hands thoroughly calloused from a day of digging, I wouldn't be sitting here contemplating a new password, Instead I would be sitting here trying to figure out how to explain to my husband why our backyard has been overrun by gophers.

Flickers & Twisters

● ● ●

I'M NOT GOING TO LIE. When I first met my husband he had a semi-full head of hair. I saw pictures of it – permed tightly, long, and bleached from the sun. Really, it wasn't a bad head of hair. My father has a nice head of hair so I wasn't anticipating the speed at which Bob would lose his. I look at pictures and I can piece together a bit of a timeline. I think it took about fifteen years.

So as the hair disappeared from his head, it popped up in other random areas. A bunch of it appeared in his ears and a little tuft made its way into his nose. What I didn't expect, though, was the amount that seemed to gather at the little area in the small of his back. Strange. I call it 'backgina' hair.

Now, I don't want to imply that men are the only ones struggling with follicular issues as they age. We women sometimes have thinning hair as well, but more often we have the appearance of *unwanted* hair. You catching what I'm throwing? You know . . . the appearance of the 'flickers and the twisters'.

Flickers are those nasty, coarse, dark-colored hairs that appear in and around your upper lip. They feel like tree trunks. I call them flickers because I can feel them with the tips of my fingers but as soon as I try to pluck them they suck themselves in faster than a geriatric gentleman's scrotum in a cold breeze. In fact, there isn't one type of tweezer on the market today to deal with a hair at the flicker stage. Believe me, I've tried.

I've purchased tiny tweezers, slanted tweezers and even medical tweezers (you know, the kind they use to remove microscopic things out of incisions) and they *still* won't grab a flicker. This issue is compounded by the fact that, by the time you're old enough to start getting flickers, your vision has deteriorated to the point where you can't see them well enough to pull them out. Which brings me to twisters . . .

Twisters are flickers gone rogue. You don't want to be caught with a twister. Twisters are hairs that are now long enough to <gag> twist. I can leave for work with a flicker and by 4 p.m. a Transformer-like metamorphosis will have occurred and I'll now have a twister.[32]

Unlike flickers, twisters are really hard to see unless they catch the light at a certain angle. I have to count on my daughter to come home and draw attention to them with the sensitivity of someone in her twenties: "My gosh, Mom! Why don't you wax?"

I DO WAX!! But I have terrible luck with estheticians. I know it isn't reasonable to ask this when I book my appointment but I feel I must. I have to ask, "How old is the person doing my waxing?" My rationale is that if *I* can't see the rogue facial hair then chances are highly unlikely that someone older than me will see it. The other day, following my wax, the young lady said to me (in her quiet, spa-like voice), "Now Judy, I'm going to turn the lights on and hand you a mirror." I was confused and actually a little terrified. What kind of spa was this? So I asked, "What for?" and she whispered breathlessly, "So you can see if I missed anything."

"Are you kidding me?" I said. "That's why *you* have that big, lighted magnifying glass and why I am coming to *you* for my wax. I don't care what you have to do, or what chemicals and tools you need to use. I need to walk out of here without my five-o'clock shadow. Okey dokey?"

And I did.

---

32 Lighter in color than the flicker. (How does that happen?)

Losing My Mind

• • •

I'M GONNA LET YOU IN on a secret – one that might explain why I'm so pre-occupied with my memory.

I'm terrified of Alzheimer's disease.

Clarification: I'm terrified of developing Alzheimer's disease.

Every time I misplace my keys or forget a name, I worry that I have early-onset dementia. It's worse when you're having a conversation with someone who probably has early onset dementia and they insist that they've told you something and then you insist that they didn't tell you.

It's like a standoff – both of you thinking, "I can't believe she didn't remember that. I wonder if she has Alzheimer's disease?"

A few years ago I had a real scare with my brain. I was producing a large event[33] and, as usual, I was filling my brain with an incredible amount of information. I was remembering every person who registered, what their needs were, who had paid and who had not paid. I was balancing on a tightrope juggling tennis balls while singing and my brain said "STOP."

I couldn't seem to form words properly. It was if they were on the tip of my tongue but I couldn't retrieve them. It wasn't exactly aphasia but something else, and it terrified me. Returning home, I went to my doctor wondering if I was suffering symptoms of a stroke or something even more sinister: Alzheimer's disease. Strangely enough, I hadn't even considered a tumor.

---

33 Sorry . . . did I forget to tell you that not only do I work part-time for an airline, but I am also a corporate event planner?

In my case, I have reason to worry. My grandmother, one of the smartest, funniest, wittiest women I know, developed Alzheimer's. She died in her 70s after spending years trapped by her brain.

Does it skip a generation? Is it like when you try to determine if your son will lose his hair prematurely and someone says, "You look at the hair of the mother's father to find out." Which is bunk because my son *is* losing his hair and my dad, who is seventy-six right now, has a beautiful head of hair. On the other hand, my husband is almost bald so apparently my son takes after his father.

I digress . . . I don't know if I'm going to develop Alzheimer's. Perhaps when you read this I already will have developed it and will be sitting in a chair parked in a hallway of some 'home' somewhere with a vacant look in my eyes. If that's the case, don't talk at me, please talk to me. Tell me funny stories and try to make me laugh. And Amy and Matthew . . . you have to promise me something: "You have to solemnly swear to pluck random chin hairs and keep my lip waxed. If my toenails grow long and colorful like a school bus, please clip them. In fact, I *love* foot massages, so maybe when you're telling me a funny story you can give me a foot massage, too. I promise you . . . I will know that you're there. Thanks in advance . . . Oh, and kids? Sorry for putting you through this."

Back to my brain. The doc ran some tests, including a CT Scan.

The result? Nada, nothing. Everything was perfect!

We chatted about the fact that we (meaning me) are not designed to keep everything in our brain, and at some point you (meaning me) have to let some of it go. Now I could do that by relying on my smart(ass) phone to keep notes, or my daily planner or something similar, or I could risk my brain 'dumping' information like it had recently. The problem with your brain overloading and deciding that control+alt+delete=dump is that you have no control of the subject matter which is dumped. It could be something important, like banking PIN codes or online passwords.

Relax Judy, don't think so much. You don't have to remember everything all of the time. WRONG. 'Remembering' was my thing. I prided myself on remembering bank account numbers from thirty-five years ago for people who are probably dead by now and never did remember their own bank account numbers. I remembered my Air Miles card number and would ambitiously rattle it off at the grocery store instead of just giving them the card. I remembered my husband's Social Insurance Number *and* driver's licence number! Why? What was the point?

My memory is my identity. I don't know how to be judicious about what I pick and choose to file away and what to write down in a book.

My memory is a timesaver. It takes only a few moments to access even the dustiest of file drawers.

My memory is a fun parlor trick, when I can remember details about someone I met fleetingly years ago. "How is your dog?" I ask, remembering that the last time we met they were worried sick about their poodle. "Did she recover? Do you still have her?" They respond with wonder and amazement. "*How* did you remember that?"

Fear motivates me to do those stupid mind-memory puzzles. Fear motivates me to play brain games. When my score is less than perfect, I worry. When my score indicates I have a 'problem area' that I could work on, I worry.

Alas, there is nothing I can do at this point. If I get it, I get it. All the worrying, ginko biloba and ginseng in the world will not keep the memory thieves from entering my brain if they really want to get inside. Those little bastards are like Ninjas, rappelling down your forehead with tiny ropes and then getting access through your nostrils into your brain. "Fall out! Get what you can and take your time . . . this gal ain't going anywhere."

My Brown-Eyed Girl

• • •

MY GRANDMOTHER WAS AN AMAZING woman. A teacher with a flair for the dramatic, she would thrill us with Shakespearean monologues and make us giggle with laughter at her over-the-top theatrics. As a little girl I would sometimes accompany her to her high school classroom and sit at the very front of the class, facing her desk. Unorthodox perhaps, but it worked. I recall being shocked that the *teacher* Grandma was quite a bit different from the *baking, reading, hooking me onto coffee at an early age* Grandma. Teacher Grandma was no-nonsense and a wee bit terrifying whereas *MY* Grandma was softness, love and laughter.

Grandma died of Alzheimer's disease in 1993 and I wrote this poem to try and express how I felt that this wonderful human being was no longer going to be a part of our lives. In fact, she had left us quite some time before.

It didn't wait until the hours of
darkness,
Or, until the first moments of
dawn.
It stole you from us in daylight,
What was going on?

Your memories slowly fading,
Your mind no longer clear.
We couldn't comprehend
Nor could any of us hear –

Your quiet cries for an answer,
A reason for your pain,
Your mind now quickly slipping.
You didn't know my name.

A teacher in an early life,
A woman with unmatched wit,
Now couldn't dial a phone number.
Why couldn't all of this quit?

Why couldn't you just fall asleep
With all of us gathered near,
And greet Grandpa in Heaven,
The one you held most dear.

No, that would be too simple.
This disease was not that kind.
Its aim was to have you suffer,
Take your dignity and your mind.

You are gone now, my beloved
Grandma.
You walk with the angels high.
We all miss you so dearly
We find ways to say goodbye

We tell stories of your yesterdays,
Your memories now ours to share.
And stop to shed a few years
When the pain seems too great to
bear.

6. Doggie Daycare

• • •

Gone to the Dogs

• • •

I NEVER WANTED A DOG.

But then I got one, subsequently fell in love and apparently lost my ability to speak like a grown-up.

"Puddin, you are mommy's boy, aren't you?"

"Come here, sweetie. Momma wants to cuddle you."

"Wiley-boo (his name was Riley), do you want some loves?"

"Ozzie-bear, sweetie pie, come to mommy."

Makes you sick, doesn't it? I never was that affectionate with my children. It wasn't that I didn't love my kids . . . but honestly, they weren't as cute as Ozzie and Riley (kidding![34])

Riley is a mixed breed Shih Tzu/Cocker/Poodle or a ShittyCockaPoo. He has a terrible underbite that makes everyone assume he's vicious but he'd never hurt a fly. In fact, he's terrified of flies and bees and butterflies and . . . you get the picture.

Ozzie is pretty much a full-breed Shih Tzu with the attitude of a small, narcissistic member of Chinese royalty. When he was little, he had huge testicles . . . HUGE! They were so large he walked with a John Wayne swagger and I believe a little piece of him died when we had him neutered. The light shone a little less brightly. I think that's when the phobias began to develop.

Ozzie is fearful of:

---

34 No I'm not and they know it . . . which makes it sad.

a) The oven
b) The iron
c) The ironing board
d) The smoke alarm

Simply . . . he's afraid of the action and the *re*action.

The roots of his fear are not unreasonable. His fear of (a) *the oven* is in direct correlation to the fear of (d) *the smoke alarm*. When (a) is turned on it sometimes results in (d) going off and it terrifies him.

The fear of the ironing board is such that when (b) *the iron* is turned on, it means that (c) *the ironing board* will get set up. He isn't afraid of the iron; he's afraid of what it may mean. Sometimes my ironing board inexplicably collapses while ironing and it, once again, scares the shit out of him.

Riley is not bereft of talent. Oh no . . . he *is* a magician.

He can sense when there are discarded feminine hygiene products within a one-kilometer radius and he will not rest until he has found them *and* paraded them amongst my dinner guests. It's like crack cocaine to him.

Case in point: Once we had people over for supper and I noticed Riley wasn't hovering near the table waiting for something to fall. I got up to discover that Riley had been dumpster diving and had discovered a hit of 'crack'. I tried to grab him but he got away and crawled under the table to hide with the 'crack' in his mouth. I was now on all fours, crawling under the table (where my guests were all seated) to wrestle the treasure out of his mouth.

Transcript (my best recollection of the event):

Me: "Come on Wiley-poo . . . come to momma. Momma has a treat, Wiley-poo."
Mother-in-Law: "What does he have? What does he have?"
Bob: "What does he have? What does he have?"
Me (trying to come up with something to say): "Oh . . . nothing, just something . . . (bangs head on table). SHIT!"

Me: "Riley! Come out right now!"

Me: "Riley! Get your ass out from under that table right now!"

Me: "Fuck!"

Mother-in-Law: "What, dear?"

Me (managing to grab Riley and drag him out with treasure dangling from mouth, opening French doors and tossing Riley – sans treasure – outside): "Whew! Chocolate can be so dangerous for dogs (wink)."

Animal House

• • •

FLASH FORWARD 10 YEARS.

Ozzie wears a wool beret that rests at a jaunty angle on his wee head. Most days you'll see him smoking a cigarillo as he leans back into the couch to study me with his big brown eyes. He has a sour disposition and is incredibly verbal with his needs. As he has aged, he has taken to depositing 'presents' on the hardwood floor. I yell at him, "Why did you do that?" and he just turns his back on me, pretending he's deaf. A skin condition, not unlike psoriasis, has robbed him of his beautiful black hair and it now is sparse and almost white in color. The medication he takes has caused a rapid, extreme weight gain, bloating his once strong, proud body into a caricature of his formal self. When I reach around his belly to help pick him up to place him in bed, he normally passes wind, with a sad "phfew-wwwww" noise – loud, sharp farting is something that he abandoned with his youth. His head turns and I imagine him saying, "The dog did it."

Riley, on the other hand, wears no clothes. Instead he wanders naked from room to room listening to the beat of his own heart. His hearing diminished from 'selective' to completely gone about two years ago and his eyes appear milky. His OCD, which was charming and funny when he was younger, is now paralyzing. He touches the food to his mouth over and over again before he takes a bite, and therefore dinnertime becomes a three-act play and he has grown thin. Fear of bees and bugs and all things flying makes sitting on the sundeck in the summer unbearable. He wants to go in, he wants to go out, he wants to go in, he wants to go out. He is 'naked and afraid'.

These are not people. These are my dogs and this is how I see them in my mind's eye.

Yes, I anthropomorphize them, but that is what makes dog ownership so much fun! It's not like I dress them up. (Okay . . . I *did* dress them up a couple of times, but just for a picture.)

These two good-looking men have been in our lives for more than a decade. They are senior dogs and believe they should be cared for in the manner to which they've become accustomed. When we camp, we bring extra chairs for them to rest their arthritic bodies on (guests can sit at the picnic table). We groom them regularly, they visit the doctor more often than we do and we (hubby and I) spend an inordinate amount of time discussing their bowel movements.

We speak to them like we would speak to children. Ozzie becomes "Oh AUUUUUHZZIE!" and Riley becomes, "What's wrong Wiley-bear?"

We even apologize to them.

Yes.

Once I jumped up from my chair (I am clearly embellishing . . . I haven't jumped for anything in a long time unless it involved Dairy Queen). Anyway, I jumped from my chair and accidentally stepped on Fatso Ozzie. Phfewwww (gas escaping) was followed by a painful yelp and he ran for safety under the table.

"I am sooooooo sorry!" I exclaim and rush to comfort him. On my hands and knees I crawl under the table to pull him out, but he is clearly fearful and trembling. I'm fairly certain he believes I did it on purpose.

I'm beside myself with guilt and want to make it up to him with cuddles and love and cooing into his stinky ear, but he won't come out from underneath the damn table!

I think to myself, "He's doing this deliberately to make me feel badly. I'm certain of it. He has always liked to play mind games!"

I climb out from under the table, which involves bumping my head and snarl, "Fine! Stay there! I don't care! Why were you sitting right underneath my chair anyway?" I walk away, abandoning him.

Riley, the people-pleaser, has been watching the entire exchange and jumps at the chance to make everything 'better'. He leaps off the blanket he was resting on and runs up to me. I bend down and he begins to lick my hand, as if to say, "We know you didn't mean it."

Tears well up in my eyes, which could be an emotional reaction to the moment or it could be a physical reaction to Riley's HORRIFICALLY bad breath.

It doesn't matter.

These are not dogs. They are tiny humans with big personalities and I love them both.

Even Ozzie.

7. Crafting Holiday Magic

• • •

Occupy Christmas

• • •

"THE FIRST FACEBOOK FRIEND WHO announces that they have their tree up, baking done, Christmas shopping done *and* wrapped, gets deleted off my Facebook friends list." There. I said it. I said what many are thinking. Who *are* these people? Where do they get their motivation, energy, time? Perhaps they store their Christmas tree fully decorated . . . hmm-mmmm? Perhaps they use <gasp> . . . frozen tart shells? Or maybe they purchase all their gifts online?

Whatever they do, I don't want to hear it. I'm what is known as a Christmastinator: someone who isn't very organized at Christmas and who tends to put a lot of pressure on herself. Years ago (how many times have I started a sentence with that?) . . . Anyway, years ago I was much more organized. I did baking galore; I made my own Irish Cream; I wrote a hilarious Christmas letter (I thought it was funny); I decorated outside with garlands and big red poinsettia flowers; I did a *theme* tree, for goodness sake! I *was* Martha Stewart (well, perhaps the Martha *before* the prison sentence).

What the heck happened? Four words: The kids left home. When you have children in your home you feel the added pressure to create a magical moment, a Hallmark memory. When it's simply your hubby and yourself, you tend to let things slide. For instance, if I can come up with a meal where canned soup is involved, that's a win for me. If he can come up with a meal where I use the stove rather than the microwave, that's a win for him.

It's not like I've abandoned the holiday. I love to craft, love to play with flower arranging, purchase all the Christmas magazines and read all the best blogs. I do end up decorating, baking and purchasing presents. I just leave it a bit . . . late, perhaps?

I think we put extra pressure on ourselves when we see Halloween candy mixed with Christmas décor. We begin wondering how our outdoor Halloween Howl display can transform into the Nativity Scene. (Don't laugh . . . I've seen it done.)

When do I start my Christmas shopping/baking/decorating? Well it's somewhere between the time when there are lots of choices available in the stores to the time where there's nothing but plastic-backed, red ribbon bows edged in glitter. It's the time when you have to go to three stores before you find tart shells, and the time when you might not receive delivery of your online order until after the holiday season.

I'm an intelligent person (my mom says so), so why would I do this to myself? Why would I prefer to operate in this nether land of diminished opportunity? I honestly don't know. Perhaps if I sat down with Oprah, Dr. Phil or Dr. Oz it would help me understand my Christmastinating ways.

My target date for Christmas décor is December 13, my target date for Christmas shopping completion is December 18, wrapping will be completed December 24, and anything left to wrap will be stuffed in an oversized, quilted stocking from 'Santa'. Baking? Well, thankfully my brother-in-law is a fabulous baker and my friend Sue always creates a basket of deliciousness for Christmas.

Don't put too much pressure on yourself. Christmas is whatever/ wherever you want it to be. It can be all of the traditional trappings, or it can be just some of them, and it doesn't need to happen overnight. We're the ninety-nine per cent.

Trick or Treat

• • •

I'LL ADMIT IT: I HAVE never, ever gone out trick or treating. No . . . *not* because I'm older than dirt and they hadn't 'invented' trick or treating when I was a child. No, I lived on a farm during those formative 'trick or treating' years and therefore it was something that just didn't happen. Don't get me wrong; I'm not upset or saddened by it and I don't think it did me any harm. Note: I've always been weirded out that society approves of us telling our three-year-old (who is dressed like a pageant winner from the TLC program *Toddlers & Tiaras*), "Now princess, sweetie pie, precious, go to the door and tell the big man that you want candy and you want it now!"

As a farm kid growing up in a rural community, we celebrated Halloween differently. We came to our small school with our costumes concealed in a black garbage bag. At precisely 1 p.m., our teachers would tell us, "Okay, time to get the costumes on" and we'd all get dressed and then do the march through all the junior and senior high classrooms. This was exciting.

Under normal circumstances these same junior and senior high school students were throwing things at us, making fun of us or tripping us on the bus. But during that golden hour on Halloween they were visibly impressed (and perhaps a little jealous that we could dress up and they no longer could). Then we'd return to our classroom where we enjoyed a party atmosphere lovingly prepared by our teachers. (Where did they find the time?) The party snacks were things like popcorn balls and candy apples (not a good choice for a farm kid without a dental plan). We bobbed for apples and decorated the windows with construction paper pumpkins. There was nothing gluten, lactose or nut free about the celebration – it is a wonder that no one lost their life from anaphylaxis or pooped their pants from a lactose reaction.

On the bus ride home the older kids would steal our candy but, never fear, my awesome bus driver had a bag of treats for each of us and would hand them to us as we got off the bus. Gosh, those were simpler times, weren't they?

Flash forward to today's world. My recollection of my childhood must seem like fiction. We live in a world where candy isn't allowed at school; a world where if a grown man offered a bag of candy to a child he might be arrested; a world where 'trick or treat' might mean something sinister; and a world where the child on your front porch may say something like, "Do you have any gluten-free, celiac-friendly, Kosher, vegan, low-carb candy?"

It doesn't make it a bad world. It just makes it a different world.

My kids are adults so I'm a bit out of the loop with some of the costumes. "You're a pretty skinny Incredible Hulk, little boy," I say. I immediately get a dirty look. "Lady, I'm the Green Hornet. Get with it!" And he stamps out his cigarette and stomps off, saying, "Come on, Mom, this lady is stupid."

Devil Thy Name is Pinterest

● ● ●

SOMETIMES I HAVE AN OVERWHELMING urge . . . to craft. I've become addicted to the online social networking site Pinterest,[35] have 'pinned' some fabulous D.I.Y. projects and was anxious to try them.

Stopping for craft supplies at Walmart, I ran into some friends in the lineup at the register. "What are you doing today, Judy?" one asked, clearly puzzled by the hodge-podge of supplies in my cart. Excitedly, I responded with, "I saw this really cool D.I.Y. on Pinterest and I'm going to go try it. I'm going to dye two white t-shirts and then with one I'll make an infinity scarf and with the other I'll make a flower embellishment." (The man's eyes had glazed over by this time but I think his wife was interested.) I was feeling pretty darn superior with my craft plans for the day. I mean, honestly, I was going to make some pretty amazing things. "If I have time afterwards, I'm going to try and make homemade marshmallows," I called out to them as they left the register.

I was fairly confident that I was going to create magic with my craft supplies. I could already see myself wearing the scarf with the matching flower and people were going to say, "Wow, that's amazing! Where did you buy it?" And I'd look at them with that Martha Stewart look – you know, the one with the tiny smile and head tilt, the look that says, 'Yes, I *am* amazing' – and say, "I made it with theeeese" and I'd stretch out

---

35 Pinterest: Online pinboard where you can organize and share things that you love www.pinterest.com.

113

my hands like a healer and they would avert their eyes out of respect. (What? It's *my* imagination and it *could* happen.)

I made a second stop at the discount store, for felt. I was going to make these amazing felt flowers that I'd seen recently at the Big City Farmers Market. They were really pretty but they cost fifty dollars! I figured I could make them myself for a fraction of the price. After collecting the felt and some embellishments, I headed home to begin crafting.

The only thing missing from my crafting day was my mom, who normally acts as confidante and spiritual advisor during my D.I.Y. projects. She is generally game for anything I'm willing to try and wisely fills in the gaps that the D.I.Y. instructions leave out. I don't know why I didn't call her to come and join me. She would have been that voice of reason, we would have had some laughs, and things might have turned out differently. In the wake of the subsequent craft disaster, I did what all good, well-adjusted adult children do . . .I blamed my mother. (Sorry, Mom).

First things first. I logged onto the D.I.Y. website that contained the instructions and dove right into the infinity scarf project. I needed to dye the fabric before I began the scarf and flower. Following the instructions carefully, I began soaking the fabric in the dye. I now could begin working on my felt flower project while the fabric was being processed.

Failure #1: Do you know how difficult it is to cut felt? Perhaps if, in a past life, my scissors hadn't been used to cut wire and perhaps the odd piece of wood, I might have been able to cut out the intricate flower pattern. Lesson learned? The beautiful felt flower brooches I saw at the Big City Farmer's Market were worth every penny of the fifty-dollar price tag.

At this point I was bored and my hand-cutting hand hurt. I am an instant gratification kind of gal and things were taking way too long. I got distracted by the reality show, *Real Housewives of New York* on the television in the living room. My dining room table was covered in bits of felt and band-aids (I got a blister from the scissors) and my kitchen was a mess. My hands were covered in blue dye (I could have been a hand model from the movie *Avatar*) and I knew it would take forever to clean up the kitchen.

Failure #2: Missed important step in fabric dyeing process. Who knew that salt was necessary? It wasn't in the D.I.Y. internet instructions (but *was* listed on the package of dye). As a result, the beautiful color that I had achieved was dull and diluted, not resembling in the least an ombre affect I wanted to achieve.

This is what irritates me the very most: when bloggers post D.I.Y. instructions but leave out the most important instruction. It's their way of saying, "We made this beautiful thing but we don't want you to be able to make it as easily *or* as beautiful." Or . . . they post uber-difficult instructions like, "After smoothing the material, grab opposite corners and bring them toward you forming a trapezoid parallelogram. Once it resembles the letter X, rub your tummy and pat your head . . ." I realize that these instructions made no sense and that's exactly my point.

So craft day ended without an infinity scarf or a beautiful felt brooch. Considering my difficulties, it's a blessing that I didn't attempt marshmallows.

I'd probably have burned the house down.

The Christmas Letter

• • •

DURING NOVEMBER AND DECEMBER THE mailbox is filled with Christmas cards, awkward family photo cards and, of course, a few Christmas letters: those generic family yearbooks, printed in a flowery font on grey-tinted cardstock, surrounded by poinsettias or snowflakes. I've written my fair share of holiday tomes and have received a few unique ones. I've received letters where they describe 'in detail' the removal of a mole, letters describing their divorce, letters that speak to their disappointment with life and the pursuit of happiness and, finally, I've received the 'brag letter'. I thought it might be fun to write a facetious/fictitious 'what not to say' Christmas letter and share it with all of you. Enjoy!

Dear family and friends:

Bonne Noelle! Whew . . . I can't believe that an entire year has passed and it will soon be 2012. I beg your indulgence – you recall that last year our family was committed to being 'green'? Well, this year we've committed to being 'Canadian' and therefore we have abandoned the traditional unilingual Christmas letter for one sprinkled with both official languages.

Where do I begin? Our youngest son Jackson has continued to amaze us with his brilliance. He has been accepted into the Médecins sans Frontiers[36] program and he is only seventeen years old! He is a little like a cheval de course[37] that one. We have a difficult time holding him back. Marteena is currently dancing The

---

36 Doctors Without Borders
37 Racehorse

Nutcracker with the Royal Winnipeg Ballet. (I have included a schedule with show times – please note that any bouquets presented to her must only contain blanc fleur.[38]) We aren't certain what her future will bring, but whatever it may be, fame will surely follow.

Frederick has been enjoying retirement…yes Retraite![39] I can barely believe that he is retired at forty-five years of age! He keeps busy with the renovations on the lake house and is committed to receiving his 'wings' before long. Surprise! Frederick is becoming a pilote.[40] Isn't that exciting? I am so very proud. Superbe![41]

Little ol' me . . . well I'm still enjoying being a soccer mom and a homemaker. Of course, we still have our housekeeper, which frees me up so that I can focus on mon travail de bienfaisance.[42] I just want to give, you know? I can't believe how much suffering there is in the world. My neighbor told me recently that they can only afford one car. One car! They have three people in their family! Frankly, I don't know how they do it.

I can't help but mention that King James Spader won the Nationals this year in Toronto. That dog is so amazing! It came down to a walk-off between him and a Shih Tzu named Duchess Lady Gaga. She probably would have won if they hadn't decided to strap on that ridiculous chapeau.[43]

I know it might be construed as bragging, but I have to share some amazing news with you. We will soon have a new addition to the family! Frederick and I have just signed the papers to buy a brand new maison![44] It is only four thousand square feet but we've already spoken to a contractor who said the frame will easily support a three-thousand-square-foot addition. Can I let you in on a secret? We got it for a song! Apparently the family who was selling had lost everything in the recent mortgage crisis. We just happened to be looking at exactly the right time. They wanted to spend one last Christmas in the house but I always think it's important to pull the band-aid off quickly. They vacated the property November

---

38 White flowers
39 Retirement
40 Do I really need to translate that one?
41 Ditto for this one
42 Charity work
43 Hat
44 House

30. We hired someone to stay in the home until January and the beginning of construction. I mean . . . we couldn't leave it empty.

I could go on and on, my life is just so great, but I should probably get these to my assistant to address and send out Postes Canada.[45]

Hugs and kisses from Frederick, Maryann, Jackson, Marteena . . . and we can't forget to include King James Spader. We are wishing you and your famille[46] *a very Merry Christmas and all the best in the coming year. Joyeux Noelle and Bonne Année.*

---

45 Canada Post
46 Family

Croquembouche or Bust!

• • •

I USED TO LOVE MARTHA Stewart. In fact, during my thirties I tried to reimagine myself as a Martha wannabe, covering Tide boxes with decoupage and brown craft paper, and wrapping all my Christmas gifts in sheets of newspaper.

To this day I owe Martha a debt of gratitude. If not for her and her daily television programs I would never have figured out how to program the VCR properly. Every day I would come home at lunch to watch the taped half-hour program where Martha would teach us how to cook the perfect omelet or fold a fitted sheet.

I admit I was envious of her wrapping room where she would transform a gift package with double-sided tape and a bone folder. Martha introduced me to washi tape and origami paper folding, envelope making and the importance of a unified color palette.

Every month I purchased her overpriced magazine, poring over each and every page for inspiration. With Martha's help, we could all become homemakers, homekeepers, or even beekeepers! We could raise organic vegetables in weed-free gardens and harvest our bounty wearing a large sunhat and oversized gauntlet garden gloves. Mosquitos didn't dare bite Martha and bumblebees buzzed around her sunhat in perfect military formation.

A large basket was always filled with flower cuttings from her glorious wildflower garden and then arranged beautifully in an antique crystal vase. A little smile would tug at the corner of her mouth when she remembered how she dazzled and confused the vendor so that he mistakenly sold it to her for half price. "One must always keeps one's wits about oneself when one is negotiating a price" she would remind us. You see, anything could be a teachable moment.

My calendar was covered with dates and times of dental appointments and teacher conferences, whereas Martha's calendar was color-coordinated and labeled magic.

January was organization month, February was all about love, March was spent looking through seed catalogues. April was Easter Eggs and Passover, May was the month to turn the mattress, June was wedding month when we were introduced to the art of letterpress. July was spent mastering the art of the perfect Pavlova so that in August it could be served with fresh berries. September was back to school and sewing name-tags into book bags, October was a special Halloween edition of *Martha Stewart Magazine*. November was cooking the perfect turkey and celebrating the sweet potato and finally, December arrived upon the gilded wings of doves specifically trained to help tie the perfect grosgrain ribbon bow.

No wonder I suffered my most severe depression during this time. The expectation that I had placed upon myself to be the perfect wife, mother and employee was now exacerbated by the onslaught of 'domestic goddess television'. Nigella Lawson and her voluptuous . . . errr . . . hair and Ina Garten with her Barefoot Contessa persona were enough to send any young mom spiraling into self-consciousness.

It was during this time that Martha introduced the entire world to the Croquembouche, pronounced KROCUMBOOSH. Basically it was a tree created out of puffed, cream-filled pastry bites. Martha didn't stop there though. No . . . Martha cut the end off a whisk and masterfully spun caramelized sugar around the tree like a filigree lace web.

SHE CUT THE END OFF THE WHISK!!

This is where I removed my apron and upped the serotonin. Like an MMA fighter I tapped out and gave up on my pursuit of perfection. I couldn't compete and didn't like the person that I was hiding inside. It was exhausting.

Twenty years later I sometimes miss my Martha moments – especially after I receive a handmade gift or a see a tablescape worthy of a Martha half-smile of satisfaction. But then I look at all of my Christmas gifts that I wrapped in half an hour using Dollar Store gift bags (apparently called the sweat pants of the gift wrapping world: They don't look great but they serve a purpose), or eat 'homemade' chicken noodle soup that I whipped up with a pre-cooked chicken I purchased from the grocery store deli, and I don't feel so bad.

Growing up and growing older is about learning when to say 'no' and when to scream STOP. It's about doing what you love and loving what you do, and embracing the shortcuts along the way.

As Martha would tell us, "It's a good thing."

My Epiphany

• • •

RECENTLY I REACHED OUT TO my Facebook friends with a comment that I was struggling with writer's block. An arrogant statement, I agree. Because, honestly, how dare I call myself a writer? Does a weekly column, a blog and an occasional CBC radio column make me a writer?

Okay, I've also written for a magazine, but it was a trade publication so I'm not sure if that counts. If a writer writes, but no one reads it, are they still a writer? I digress (as per usual). The whole "Who am I?" conversation is best continued with my therapist.

So, looking for a little distraction and perhaps some divine inspiration, I reached out on Facebook and typed the two words 'writer's block' over and over and over again, almost filling the entire status area. Describing it to you now, it was reminiscent of a scene you might see in a horror story where the detective reads the crazy person's diary, or maybe something from a Stephen King novel (continuous comparisons to real writers makes me feel better): "All work and no play makes Jack a dull boy."

Dipping my toe in crazy town.

Yup.

So I turned off my computer and walked away. Got a coffee. Watched some television. Decided to try again.

I opened my laptop and heard this loud buzzer noise. (For those without a Mac computer, it sounds like the buzzer from Family Feud . . . the one where the big X appears to indicate a wrong answer.)

The buzzing sound reminded me of something!

Sure enough, the little square in the corner with the clock was there and it said, "REMINDER TOMORROW: EPIPHANY."

Oh.My.Goodness. Is this the law of attraction at work? Is this the divine inspiration that I was reaching for?

I had cleaned my home office over the weekend and I remember throwing out that old DVD, *The Secret*. Should I go through the garbage and find it again?

My second instinct was cynicism. Was this some terrifying computer virus attacking my hard drive? Did I catch something from downloading something that I found on Pinterest (Devil's playground)?

I posted the experience on social media and a friend responded that he also had received the reminder of an impending epiphany on his laptop that morning and wondered what was happening.

Hmmm. Curiouser and curiouser.

The online dictionary describes an epiphany as being "a sudden, powerful, and often spiritual or life-changing realization that a character experiences in an otherwise ordinary moment." Holy shit! Now I was intrigued.

Why did I have to wait until the next day?

I was so excited! Finally I was going to have something really **BIG** to write about. I admit that I had side-eyed longingly at other writers who had really complex dysfunction in their bag of tricks to pull from.

I wanted to call my mom and say, "Remember how I was a little disappointed that my childhood was normal and that I was a little sad that there was no one with (air quote) 'problems' from which I could draw inspiration? Well . . . no worries, because TOMORROW I am scheduled to have an epiphany!"

All day I wondered, what would it be like? I couldn't remember the last time I had an epiphany. I mean . . . a revelation, yes, . . . but epiphany? No. No epiphanies.

That night I went to bed relatively early. I was excited. It was like Christmas Eve and I already knew that I was getting something special!

Rising at seven in the morning, I tried to pace myself. It isn't every day that a girl wakes up knowing she's going to experience an epiphany.

I turned the furnace up a bit and made a pot of coffee while stumbling around with a goofy smile on my sheet-creased face. It was my 'remember this moment forever because your life is going to change after you experience the epiphany' face.

I poured my coffee and added the milk, not bothering to stir them together, and headed for my big, cozy, living room chair. I pulled up the ottoman where I could rest my freakishly short legs that would otherwise dangle without purpose.

Pausing . . . taking it all in: the Christmas tree still up and decorated in the corner of the room, the popcorn bowls from last night resting on the coffee table, the stain on the carpet where one of the dogs had made a 'boo-boo'.

In a few seconds none of it will matter. I will have experienced my epiphany.

Deep breath Judy, deep breath. I opened my computer and waited. And waited. And waited. Nothing.

What was going on? Was this some type of cruel joke?

So I Googled 'epiphany' and it popped right up.

Apparently there are multiple definitions of epiphany.

Today was January 6th.

I wasn't going to *have* an epiphany. Today *was* the Epiphany.

A Christian observance, the Epiphany *is* a pretty big deal.

Well played Macbook, well played. No hard feelings.

Side Note: Perhaps I should look into attending Sunday School? Hey! Is THAT my epiphany?

8. Lions, Tigers and Hormones . . . Oh My!

. . .

Sudden Sensitivity to Stupid

• • •

THE FOLLOWING WAS LISTED ON a website under *Additional Peri-Menopause Symptoms:*

" . . . other symptoms, which are related to peri-menopause and they can vary depending on the individual. But generally speaking they include: weight gain, breast tenderness, stress, lack of energy, fatigue, dull and thinning of hair, dry skin, wrinkles and fine lines, mood swings, irritability, depression, migraine and headaches, urine leakage, urinary urgency, decreased libido, insomnia, and last but not least irregular periods . . ."

Are you fucking kidding me?

Seriously?

These are the symptoms which I have noticed:

Sensitivity to Stupid:[47] Not everyone can be a genius and I'm in no way implying that I am, but stupidity kills (as evidenced by those folks who posthumously receive the Darwin Awards[48] each year) and if simply being in their 'bubble' somehow increases the probability that I will meet an untimely death? Well . . . I'm not gonna chance it.

Decreased ability to bring myself to say something nice: I give nice where nice is due. What I don't do any longer is pander.[49]

---

47 People who are as dumb as a bag of hair.
48 http://www.darwinawards.com
49 Kiss someone's ass.

Inability to wait for cashier to quit texting her boyfriend so she can ring my purchases through: Do you hear that? That was church bells ringing . . . customer service is dead.

Dislike standing in line: Unless there are Michael Bublé tickets *or* bellinis waiting for me at the end of said line.

Inability to respond without force to someone who honks their horn while they are behind me. This applies while driving and while walking. I will cut you....yes I will.

Fixation with the entire *Real Housewives* franchise.

Inability to watch Justin Beiber without wanting to comb his hair back away from his face and pull up his pants.

Do I Need a Tinfoil Hat?

• • •

I'M PRETTY SURE MY HUSBAND can read my mind.

Case in point:

Bob: "Where are you going?" (circling you as you put your coat on, kinda like a puppy thinking that he might get a ride in the car).

Me: "Going to run a few errands" (keeping my tone and pitch even as if *I am* speaking to a puppy and not sure where I'm going, as long as it is an hour away from him because he's driving me insane).

Bob (still circling): "Are you going grocery shopping?"

Me (not sure how to answer that question): "Ummmmmm . . . maybe?"

Bob: "Can I come?"

Me (shoulders drooping): "Sure honey . . . haha . . . I would *love* to have you come with me.[50]"

Perhaps too much emphasis on *love.*

Bob (no longer circling, smile fading, hopes for a car ride diminishing): "If you don't want me to come, just tell me you don't want me to come."

---

50 In fact...lets make a day of it. Let's start with lunch, then shopping, followed by the movies where we can sit side by side, perhaps hold hands, followed by cuddling on the couch.

Me (voice raising slightly, indicating that I'm lying): "No, come with me. Really, I want you to come."

Bob: "You obviously don't want me to come. I'm staying home."

Me (hidden relief bubbling up inside): "Fine! Do whatever you want, but don't make it sound like you weren't asked.[51]"

---

51 Jedi mind control technique.

Call Me Crazy If You Want

• • •

I HAVE A LITTLE BIT of OCD. I affectionately call myself "un peu" crazy.

I am what is known as a *Checker*. I have an overwhelming need to *check* things.

Doors, water taps, stovetops, irons, coffee-makers . . .

I check to make sure that the doors are locked, water taps are turned off, stoves are not left on, irons are not left plugged in, coffee-makers are turned off and not left on a hot burner.

I think the world needs people who check.

- We always know how many miles to the next gas station.
- We are always at the airport at least two hours before an international flight.
- We are ten minutes early for appointments.

We are the ones who read life's instructions and keep those around us from hurting themselves. We watch the in-flight safety demonstration so that we can guide you to the nearest exit after the crash. We will remember that there is a flotation device located *under* our seat and will calmly put on your oxygen mask before we put on our own. You want to place us mid-cabin or at the emergency exits. People like us save lives!

Looking at the list: Doors, water taps, stovetops, irons, coffee-makers . . . a psychiatrist might say that I have a fear of fire (arsonphobia) and perhaps drowning (aquaphobia).

I also suffer from arachnophobia (fear of spiders), agrizoophobia (fear of wild animals, specifically bears[52]), apiphobia (fear of bees), acrophobia (fear of heights), misophonia (hatred of some sounds) and of course . . . duh . . . atomosophobia (fear of atomic explosions).

Don't pity me. I'm perfectly comfortable bobbing in the shallow end of the crazy pool with my water wings. I've developed brilliant coping techniques.

I take pictures! Currently I have about a thousand photos on my phone that have been taken before I leave the house. I take pictures of the taps in the kitchen so I know that they are in the off position. I take pictures of the bottom of the sink to ensure that the plug is not anywhere near the drain (a dripping sink into a plugged drain would spell disaster). No....I don't have a leaking tap, but it COULD HAPPEN. I take a picture of the unplugged coffee pot that has been positioned far away from its normal place of use so that it cannot somehow fire up again. I take a picture of the stove dials to ensure they are in the locked and off position. Whew! That's just the kitchen! I do the same in the bathroom and the coup de grace is when I take a photo of the deadbolt turned in the lock confirming the home is secure.

I know what you're thinking. You're thinking . . . "That girl is brilliant!"

I'm just doing what I have to do to maintain my sanity, but I appreciate the kind thoughts.

Recently I've found that if I'm not the last person out of the home, somehow I waive all paranoid delusions. It is as if, when I'm not personally responsible, I don't have to carry the burden with me.

I let Bob lock up.

---

52 Do you blame me?

The Happy Hugger

• • •

NOTE: WHILE THIS SPECIFIC CONVERSATION did not actually happen, a variation of it has happened many, many times. I'm simply using my ability to 'over-embellish' and taking some artistic license because . . . well, that's what I do.

Carry on.

"What's wrong, Mom?" The worry and fear is clearly audible in my daughter's voice.

"Nothing is wrong! Why do you assume something is wrong?" I muffle in response.

"Because you're hugging me, that's why! Tell me Mom, tell me . . . Did something happen to one of the dogs?" Amy wriggles out of my awkward embrace to look (down) me in the eyes. (She's five-foot-five and I'm five-foot-one.)

"NOTHING HAPPENED TO ANYONE OR ANYTHING! Can't a mother hug her child for no apparent reason?" Now I'm beginning to get irritated *and* I'm feeling a hot flash coming on.

Breaking into gut-busting laughter, Amy almost folds in half, hugging her midsection. "HAHAHAHA . . . ummmmm . . . in your case, no! In this family we go to Dad or Grandma for hugs. We know you're not a touchy-feely person and it's fairly obvious you were uncomfortable. Hugging me right now. Is this sudden attempt to be demonstrative a 'menopause' thing?"

"No it is *not* a menopause thing. Maybe I'm turning over a new leaf! Perhaps I'm trying to step outside my emotional comfort zone,"

I respond, frustrated that my lack of hugging experience is now affecting my performance. Also . . . why does everyone blame everything on menopause!

Sigh . . .

She is correct.

I am *not* a hugger.

I freely admit it.

Hugging makes me uncomfortable because there are so many things to consider. I overthink it.

Side hug or full frontal?

Both arms or just one?

How long should it last?

How do I know when it's over?

At what point does it become creepy?

Believe me, I consider everything. During a long hug my mind will sometimes wander: "Milk, eggs, bread . . ."

My family knows when a hug with me is over as I 'double-tap' to signal that we should break. Or, I've been known to begin swaying from side to side because, honestly, how long can two people stand there . . . just . . . hugging.

I asked my friends the following questions: Do you enjoy hugging? How long should a hug last? How do you know when a hug is over? How tight should a hug be? Is there different hugging compression based on the reason for the hug? The answers were amazing and I have to share them with you. The responses are evidence that I have some very cool friends. I'm just sayin' . . .

"In and hug . . . three seconds . . . out. The closer the friendship, the tighter the hug. Except when it's so tight you crack someone's rib. Oops . . ."

"I love hugging! Because I'm short, for most adults I fit right under their chin. If I turn my head sideways I can hear their heartbeat. I hug for a full inhale and exhale, or less if I feel them release the squeeze or move the feet. Loved ones get a good squeeze, friends a light one, acquaintances is just arms, no body. I can seriously feel the stress leave my body from a good hug!"

"*Hugs are incredible! Everyone needs a hug once in a while. Hugs can be quick expressions of gratitude, thanks, comfort or just a playful 'How are you?' Deep down inside we all like receiving and giving hugs. Let your inner hugger out!*"

"*I LOVE HUGS . . . four hugs a day to survive, eight hugs a day for maintenance, and twelve hugs a day for growth.*"[53]

"*The kinds of hugs depend on the meaning. 1. Side hugs for casual acquaintances; 2. Front hug using arms but the only body contact is chest and shoulders, used as a greeting for close friends; and, 3. Full body hug for those special people in your life.*"[54]

"*Love, love, love, hugs! Hugs release pleasure and happy hormones and just make us feel good. Oh yes there are many types of hugs for all types of situations! I love hugs! Hug me any time! Except not the bone-crushing kind. Those aren't nice!*"[55]

So there you have it. Proof positive that I need to embrace hugging because it will make me happier, and make those around me feel loved. Try it for yourself!

---

53 Hashtag #Blessed

54 This individual loves to overthink the situation – fairly certain he or she is related.

55 When I read this one I imagine that it is said after sucking helium from a balloon.

Put That Apple Down, Walk Away, and No One Gets Hurt!

• • •

I DID A RANDOM POLL recently with my friends. I asked, "Does the sound of your husband eating make you angry?"

Surprisingly *all* of them responded with an emphatic "*Yes!*" In fact, it didn't just make them angry, it enraged them.

They all thought it was a sign that their marriage was failing.

No! I reassured them, it's not failing. We all suffer from 'misophonia', which is a hatred of sound!

That's why the sound of mouth breathing or apple biting or carrot eating elicits such rage. We used to tolerate the noise but as we age we begin to tackle it passive aggressively. Comments like, "THAT sounds like you are enjoying it."[56] or "Hahaha! Pace yourself. There are other apples." <gag>.

After years of hearing the SNAP of a carrot followed by the loud chewing, we abandon all sense of kindness and tolerance and we begin to get nasty.[57]

"MUST YOU eat that here? MUST YOU chew that loudly?" we say, rolling our eyes and sighing loudly.

With hurt feelings, our partner says something like, "If you don't like it, then leave the room," and then proceeds to take the biggest, noisiest bite from the apple.

---

56 You are eating like a pig.
57 Violent

Now you can tell them, "I have a disease, don't mock me."

I have even written a Valentine's Day poem for those who suffer from misophonia:

Roses are red
Violets are blue
When you leave the room when you are eating a raw carrot
because the sound instantly makes me angry
That's nice. Thank you.

Misophonia . . . look it up . . . it's real.

9. Standards of Measurement

• • •

My Piece of String

• • •

I'M GOING TO ADMIT SOMETHING. I don't really know how to use a measuring tape properly. I mean, of course I know how to physically use the tape; it's the reading of the tape that causes me (and those around me) so much angst.

Case in point: When I was asked to measure my front door for my husband, who was in the big city looking for a replacement door, I responded with, "It looks like it's thirty-one and then eight . . . no, maybe nine little lines."

Then I think I heard a scream . . . probably a coyote or something.

He didn't pick up a door that day.

My feeling is that the only people who need to use sixteenths or thirty-seconds are NASA folks and perhaps people who build prosthetic limbs. Everyone else is just showing off.

Apparently I'm wrong. You can't build a piece of furniture and tape a package of gum to it and call it a 'leveling kit'.

Little ol' me has no need to venture that far into the fraction world.

It does not go unnoticed that I have not fully embraced the metric system yet, either. I'm not math illiterate, but I'm not a savant, either. I'm somewhere in the middle with momentary flashes of brilliance and small gaps of ineptitude. The measuring tape thingy falls into one of the gaps.

I have other strengths. As a troubleshooter, I can come up with ways (coping mechanisms) to deal with my measuring tape issues:

* I could use a string and take said string down to the hardware store!
* I could take a marker and put a little dot on the measuring tape and then take the tape with me to the store!
* I could take a picture of the marked-up measuring tape, clearly showing the measurement, and then show the picture to the helpful folks at the hardware store!

I just heard another scream . . .

I'm not the only person in the world who struggles with reading a measuring tape. I recall that my automotive instructor friend would teach a 'reading measuring tape' class at the beginning of the school year. I'm certain he did it to save his own sanity.

Considering my shortcomings, one would think that I'd be more empathetic toward those who also have difficulty with problems involving math.

I *am* empathetic, unless it verges on the ridiculous . . .

Recently, a very good friend of mine relayed a story to me and gave me permission to share it with all of you.

'Jane' was catering a meal for a large group of people and needed to pre-order some buns from a bakery.

Jane approached the bakery counter and was assisted by a smiling, young bakery employee. Let's listen in . . .

Jane: "I need to pre-order some buns for an event next week."

Bakery employee: "No problem. How many would you like to order?"

Jane (refers to her guest list and does some calculating in her head): "I think I should order about 175 or 180. Let's do 180. Then I'll have some extra."

Bakery employee: "We sell them by the dozen, so I'll have to figure that out."

The young bakery employee proceeds to bring out her calculator and begins calculating while Jane looks on.

12 x 6? Nope . . . shakes her pretty head.

12 x 7? Nope . . . shakes it again.

12 x . . .

STOP!

Jane (baffled by what she's seeing, looks around to see if she's on a *Just for Laughs* program, but seeing no cameras, she now begins to speak very slowly to the young employee): "Perhaps if you take 180 and divide it by 12, you'll come up with the answer."

Bakery employee (big smile on her face because she has now learned a 'trick'): "It's fifteen! You need fifteen dozen buns."

Jane: "I need half to be whole wheat and half to be white."

Bakery employee writes down fifteen whole wheat and fifteen white.

Jane (no longer interested in continuing with the teachable moment): "No . . . I don't need 360 buns. Just give me eight dozen whole wheat and eight dozen white."

I think I just heard some screams . . . coyotes again?

First World Problems

● ● ●

FIRST WORLD PROBLEM: DEFINED IN the Urban Dictionary as "problems from living in a wealthy, industrialized nation that Third World folks would probably roll their eyes at."

Statements such as, "OMG, my satellite dish won't support my third television!" or complaining that "We're all out of soy milk! I hate it when I have to drink two-per-cent."

These are all First World problems.

I admit I get caught up in the whole 'poor me' thing sometimes and I should probably feel ashamed of myself. Except, the First World just happens to be *my* world and, petty as it may be, those things (not exactly those things, but things like them) affect me.

For example:

Some travel etiquette tips that I have learned in my travels . . .

Su seatback es mi seatback: Just because the seatback reclines a long way doesn't mean that you should recline it all the way. If I can see your hair plugs or hear the music coming out of your iPod ear buds because YOU HAVE RECLINED ONTO MY LAP – then perhaps it is a bit too far.

Bag ladies: Many of us carry large purses and we like to carry them over our shoulders. Unfortunately, when we board the plane with them over our shoulders, we tend to hit all the seated passengers on the head as we move down the aisle to our seat. Carry your Prada Coach knockoff bag in front of you.

We will eventually *all* get off the aircraft. The plane has reached the gate but the door hasn't opened yet. If you're in seat 37B, stay the fuck in your seat.

Personal hygiene: I'm impressed that you're committed to oral hygiene, but flossing your teeth while sitting next to me kinda grosses me out (really happened). Likewise for clipping your toenails (didn't happen to me, but would be equally gross).

Are You a Prowling Lion?

● ● ●

FOR ME, BELIEVING IN THE law of attraction is a little like believing in Santa Claus. You know it's ninety-nine per cent bullshit but there's a teeny, tiny part of you that thinks, "Maybe if I really believe . . ." So you still write the letters (buy the books), put the cookies out (hire a life coach), but deep down you know that it's a pile of crap.

Ask yourself:

Are you an 'upward bound' thinker?

Perhaps a 'prowling lion'?

Do you need a 'life coach'?

What about the 'Law of Compensation'?

The Law of Compensation applies when *you* pay a life coach to tell you things, which *you already know.* The only difference is that they might tell you in fifteen-minute installments over six months at a low, low price of $59.99 per installment.

I don't want to paint the whole bunch with an invisible, magic brush operated by my thoughts, but there are a certain number of those people who are just taking advantage of folks.

Here are Judy's Rules for Happiness:

* Value yourself.
* Laugh often.
* Smile.
* Work Hard.
* Learn to say you're sorry.

* Cuddle a puppy.
* Quit breaking your pills in half; they work better if you take as prescribed.

Or tell the assholes in your life the following: "I'm not an interior designer or a life coach, but I'm pretty sure that my emotional feng shui would improve if you would leave my fucking line of sight."

Namaste, folks . . . Namaste.

The Apocalypse is Coming!
The Apocalypse is Coming!

• • •

DID YOU READ THE CHAPTER about the Law of Attraction? If you didn't read that chapter, let's recap:

For me, believing in the law of attraction is a little like believing in Santa Claus. You know that it's ninety-nine per cent bullshit but there is a teeny, tiny part of you that thinks, "Maybe if I really believe . . ."

The same can be said about the Apocalypse. Yes, it *could* happen, but WTF am I going to do about it if it is and, more importantly, what do I wear?

Some say that a space ship will land and only a certain number of 'believers' (not to be confused with 'Beliebers', although a certain number of them are batshit[58] crazy enough) will be invited on board.

What do you wear if that were to happen? Apparently blue tracksuits and white runners. Considering there are 144,000 of them and space is probably at a premium, it might be a good idea to bring a long-lasting deodorant.

Important to remember: Do *not* drink the kool-aid.

There is a small group on the planet who believe we will experience a 'Zombie' Apocalypse. If it were to occur, and you wanted to pack a 'go bag', you probably could get away with the shabby chic look and fit right in. Think . . . grubby Olsen twins.

---

58 Tinfoil hat crazy

The sky is falling? Well, Chicken Little certainly made an ass of himself by saying it but I guess it could happen. What to pack? Gravity boots.

Crazy didn't just happen in the twenty-first century. There have been many, many books about Armageddon. Here is an example:

88 Reasons Why the Rapture will be in 1988 by Edgar C. Whisenant. He wrote a follow-up book, *The Final Shout: Rapture Report 1989* which probably could have been followed by *Dying of Embarrassment: the Edgar Whisenant Story.*

When you think about it logically, if you write a book about the Apocalypse and it actually happens like you say it will . . . there will be no speaking tour, no increase of your book exposure on Amazon.

I'm waiting for the television networks to create a reality show about the Apocalypse. Perhaps, *Redneck Rapture, Doomsday Designer, Second Coming/Second Chances* or, finally, *What Not to Wear: Apocalypse Episode.*

These might be the descriptions when you press 'info' on the cable receiver:

Doomsday Designer – Two zany designers battle it out to create the most chic underground shelter. Chad likes to incorporate the use of color, whereas Hildi is in love with feathers. Who will win? Tune in to find out.

Second Coming/Second Chances – A story of heartache, a story of love. Watch as twins, separated as small children, reconnect in advance of the Second Coming. You don't want to miss this touching episode.

What Not To Wear: Apocalypse Episode – Watch as Stacey and Clinton help Maria, a color-blind lawyer from Orange County who recently lost fifty pounds and doesn't know how to dress her new body. Maria will discover that just because the world is ending doesn't mean she can't still look professional.

Don't judge me.

Serenity NO

• • •

"OKAY CLASS! WE'RE GOING TO begin our day with some quiet reflection," says the instructor of our personal development workshop.

Judy (looks worried and begins to repeat in her head): Uh oh . . . please don't ask me to meditate, please don't ask me to meditate, please don't ask me to meditate, please don't . . .

"We're going to sit quietly and meditate."

Judy: Doh!

"Make yourselves comfortable in your chair, planting your feet firmly on the floor beneath you, hands sitting gently on your legs, shoulders square, chin up . . ."

Judy: Sure! Easy for the tall dude to say. He isn't five feet tall with twenty-nine-inch legs! I *cannot* sit comfortably unless it's a primary school desk. My legs cannot touch the floor unless I sit uncomfortably at the edge of my seat. Otherwise my feet dangle and swing, creating an obvious distraction to my 'meditation'.

Thankfully, I'm wearing my Birkenstock sandals and therefore I can sit back into my seat and let my sandals slip off my feet so that the tips touch the floor, but my toes hook around the strap, creating an extension of my leg.

I'm fairly certain that my toes can hang on for the thirty seconds or so of quiet reflection.

"Okay folks, now I'd like you to close your eyes and focus on your breathing".

Judy: Did I lock my car? I'm sure I locked my car . . . I wonder if . . .

"Breathe in through your nose and exhale from your mouth."

Judy: I wonder what they're serving for lunch?

"Now I'd like you to think about your (insert something to think about here)."

Judy: Opens one eye to look at the instructor. It has obviously been more than thirty seconds – feeling uncertain about where this 'meditation' is going.

The instructor's voice is quiet and soothing, his eyes are closed and he has this serene, focused look on his face.

Judy: Darnit! My toes can't hang onto my sandals much longer. No, they're definitely falling off! Hang on toes! It can't be long now. You can do it!

THUNK

and then . . .

THUNK

Both shoes are now underneath my chair and my feet are swinging freely.

"Now I want you to think about (insert something else here)."

Judy: I thought meditation was supposed to clear my mind. Seems like all I'm doing is filling it up with more thoughts. I open my eyes slightly and scan the room. Everyone is participating and look like they are really into this. No . . . the dude over there is clearly sleeping. Lucky guy.

Four minutes have passed. This is beginning to feel like an uncomfortable hug.

After the instructor speaks there is a gap of silence and I wonder if it means we are completed and I begin to hope . . .

"Let's imagine . . ."

Judy: OH MY GOODNESS! Let's imagine a coffee break, shall we?

I see a woman to my right shift uncomfortably in her chair and I'm fairly certain her eyes are flickering.

Aha! I'm not the only one who needs for this to end.

"Breathe in . . . breathe out."

Judy: Yay! It sounds like we're almost finished!

"Now, consider for one moment . . ."

Judy: Seriously? This is now longer than my last labor and frankly it's entirely more painful . . .

"Alright now class, we're going to slowly begin to open our eyes, focusing on our breathing and our moment of reflection."

Judy: Okay, *this* I can do. I open my eyes and look around the room and see serenity and peace.

"How was that exercise?"

Judy: Perfect . . . awesome . . . thanks. I feel amazing!

10. Suddenly Seeking Social

• • •

My Open Letter to Friends on Facebook

• • •

Dear Facebook Friends:

I get Facebook, I really do.

In fact, I enjoy using Facebook and find it challenging to come up with pithy status updates that my sarcastic, witty friends might enjoy. I like to see pictures, links to interesting news items and laugh out loud when you post videos of babies laughing or intricately choreographed first dances at weddings.

I will admit that I liberally sprinkle my posts with the happy face emoticon but try my best to restrict the use of LOL.

But that's where it ends. I have limits and I thought you did, too. Was I wrong?

Friends don't ask you to join the Mafia or help work the farm (although I do appreciate the sentiment when you share your Slotomania luck).

FYI? I don't play word games or spin the big wheel. I don't dash with diamonds, raise backyard monsters or have ever been interested in building my own Gnome Town so that I could raise beautiful butterflies. I will never, ever poke you on purpose and finally, I will not send out the yellow rose of friendship or pass it along on your behalf.

I will not challenge our friendship by requesting that you "cut and paste and post my update on your status" and will not threaten everyone by announcing that I am "cleaning out my list of friends."

I won't do those things.

Sincerely,

Judy ☺

PS: I won't correct your speling if yu don't chorect myne.

My Life in Facebook Status Updates

• • •

I USE FACEBOOK QUITE A bit. Okay, a lot. I use Facebook as my personal Tumblr. Here are a few of my 'deep' thoughts that I have shared.

Eating in restaurants after turning 50: I guess I'm getting old. The restaurant was so dark I thought it was closed. Apparently it was mood lighting :) It's called 'age profiling'. Young, hip, trendy restaurants keep the lights turned down so that the older, less hip, less trendy customers will assume the place is closed and go to the Waffle House instead :)

• • •

Martha Stewart TV show CANCELLED! I was soooo looking forward to her 2012 Christmas special, *Apocalypse Wow.*

• • •

Deep thoughts by Judy: As I made a running jump into my bed (as I almost have to do every night because it's freakishly high (Princess and the Pea high . . . and we all know which one is the princess), I realize that my next bed purchase will need to take into consideration the following: (a) Is it bionic hip friendly? (b) Can I attach railings? And finally, (c) What the heck is my sleep number?

• • •

Following some upheaval in my life: Thank goodness we're going to get back to normal. My third eye has fallen out of alignment with my chakra and it will take a lot of downward dogs to get it back into its rightful place. Namaste . . . Namaste.

● ● ●

I will begin watching hockey when (a) they throw in occasional triple axles, (b) when they include an interview question like the Miss Universe pageant or (c) someone gets a final rose, a la *The Bachelor.*

● ● ●

Quilting: Cutting perfectly fine pieces of material up into small pieces and then sewing them together again. Not.going.to.do.it

● ● ●

Things which cause me to hate Martha Stewart: When she uses the word "tipple" and when she shares a recipe that uses . . . "only Meyer Lemons." #wherecanyoubuymeyerlemons?

● ● ●

After gathering up garbage that has blown all over the yard: Why is it only apocalyptically windy on garbage day?

● ● ●

Just had someone tell me that they . . . "live gregariously through their children." I almost snorted coffee out of my nose. #wrongword #grammarpolice

● ● ●

The 'scent' from the guy standing way to close to me in the Wal-mart line smells faintly of day-old chicken.

• • •

After a stressful day at work: I find it extremely, extremely helpful when people give me guidance on 'where I can go' . . . and the things I can do to myself when I get there. So very helpful.

• • •

Relaxing on a Friday night: Hillbilly Handfishin' on television and a glass of chardonnay . . . like I won the lottery or somethin'.

• • •

Do you ever think that the day warrants attaching a warning label to yourself? What would yours be? I'm particularly fond of "Danger: be aware that frequent flareups are possible. Maintain a safe distance at all times."

• • •

Can you imagine if there was a country called 'Euphoria'?

• • •

I'm still waiting for the day when the math problem that began with "Bus A left the station at ten o'clock going one hundred miles per hour, and Bus B . . ." has any relevance to real life. #Ihatewordproblems

• • •

So . . . just thinking out loud . . . what kind of exercise regimen would be involved if I wanted to train to be a Jedi? I mean . . . probably squats, right? And maybe a bit of cardio?

• • •

I have to laugh at the jewelry store commercials on TV around Christmas – "Say it with diamonds" . . . You know I'd be cool with "saying it with vacuuming" or "saying it with cooking dinner for a change" or "saying it by putting the seat down."

• • •

Overheard at liquor store after clerk asks customer if he wants to purchase one of those plush bears for charity and he says, "My wife looks after that shit" and then says "She picks up dead people for a living." {mic drop}

• • •

clickbait "She poured coffee into her travel mug and you will not believe what happened next!" Click . . . And she spread happiness o'er the world #thatiswhathappenswhenIgetcoffee

• • •

My recollection of a particularly disturbing dream: In my dream last night I'm walking downtown during lunch hour and see a busy restaurant. Just out the front door is a man in a suit who had tripped off the roof (don't know why, it's a dream and no normal applies), hung himself and he was just hanging there. I'm angry and I say to the restaurant owner, "There's a guy hanging outside your door!" And he says, "I know. I called the police but they're really slow to respond. I thought, why should I have to lose business because they're slow? So I opened up. It doesn't seem to bother people." Meanwhile I'm trying to tweet Jonny Wakefield[59] to come and take pictures but for some reason my tweets don't go through. Ughhhh! Moral to story: Don't eat spicy food before bed.

• • •

'SHITS': They are in you to give #giveashit. If everyone gave just one shit each day for something that matters, the world would be a better place #ITookTheGiveAShitPledge

• • •

American Apparel . . . a store that I normally do not frequent, but it was necessary due to an item on a Christmas list. What can I say about American Apparel but that there is something off with their clothing line? When you enter the store it's as if you're walking with either a rock in your shoe or you've broken a heel, because everything feels like it is sitting at an irregular angle. Almost as if it's where ugly fabric goes to die and angry, hungry LA waifs (made in LA) cut out material with safety scissors and then rush to sew them together without cutting off the dangling threads.

• • •

The bar has been set to a new height! I just fell at Safeway *so spectacularly* that I expected to hear a Russian judge scream "10!" and then be whisked away for drug testing. My trip up (or down) whilst carrying a full bas-ket of grocery stuff began with navigation between a bleeping palette where I caught my foot on the wood and stumbled, gaining momentum before I said "f-it" and gave in to the experience. At this point I fell hard,

---

59 Local reporter for local newspaper.

groceries tumbling, pride and knees bruising. A very nice lady picked up groceries, another lady asked if I was all right, and a nice man gave me a hand to my feet. He exclaimed that I could have "broken a hip" but thankfully I knew that my fat assery protected my hips.

● ● ●

MOVEMBER – the month where many men resemble 1970s porn stars. #moustache #boomchickawowwow

● ● ●

And so it begins – the game of weather one-upmanship played by Northern Canadians for at least four months of the year:

"We got about three inches of snow last night."

"Really? We got at least four at our place."

"Well, the three inches we got drifted across the highway, making it seem like it was worse."

"Yeah? The four inches of snow we got was followed by freezing rain."

"Hmmmmm . . . we got freezing rain *first*, *then* the three inches of blowing, drifting snow."

"Wow! . . . Well, my car barely started."

"Really? Hmmmm . . . thankfully I have a big heated garage."

Game – Set – Match

● ● ●

The upside of not getting in to get a lip wax this week means that I can create a Halloween costume by hanging a sign around my neck that says, 'Movember - Week 1'.

● ● ●

When Bob says to me, "Remember not to use my name" (in a column or a blog) and I respond with, "That ship sailed a *long* time ago, honey."

• • •

After drinking terrible coffee using our in-room coffeemaker and only realizing on the last day that there was a Tim Horton's across the road: The in-room coffeemaker sputters and spits, steam rising from the full cup of Starbucks coffee. Although freshly brewed, the so-called "medium roast pike place" smells acrid and burnt. I lean over the cup, inhaling long and slow. "Ahhhhh Cathy, do you know what that smells like? That is the scent of disappointment." FYI - Crappy coffee Sheraton, crappy coffee . . .

• • •

While at my first Writers' Conference: Spotted my first clog wearer of the writers' conference. Oh . . . and I've found where all the banana clips went from the 1980s.

• • •

Bob saw a large garter snake while out walking in the bush. He now has taken up stamp collecting and joined a yodelling club. #nosnakesthere #safer #stayinside

• • •

At first I thought it was a ghost, but then I realized that Bob was wearing camo. #ICanHearHimButNotSeeHim

• • •

Bob's phone begins 'pinging' loudly. So I ask, "What's that?" He says, "I'm tracking a shark" (he has a new iPhone). Pinging gets louder and I say, "Is the shark outside right now?"

• • •

In the wake of the Ashley Madison dating site scandal: I thought Ashley Madison was a furniture place . . . doesn't it sound like a furniture place?

• • •

The week before Thanksgiving: Bob and I having a conversation about the fact that we've never cooked a fresh turkey. Instead, we've always have purchased a frozen one from the grocery store. Bob says, "We should try a fresh one sometime." To which I respond, "I dislike eating a turkey so fresh that its family is still grieving the loss. I prefer that some amount of time has passed and they've quit lighting candles at the hen house and eating casseroles provided by the neighbors. Makes me feel a bit less guilty when I stuff it with bread bits and onion."

• • •

I used a fraction in casual conversation today. #smartgirlmoment

• • •

I saw a leaf blow past the window of the office and I got a bit sad, thinking about summer turning to fall. Then it flitted back and I thought, "Leaves can't do that!" and realized it was a confused butterfly.

• • •

If we could quilt using glue, then I might consider it.

• • •

I just swallowed my temporary crown. Yes, I did just do that. I'm sure I shouldn't be trusted to leave my home without a helmet these days . . .

• • •

My update after reading about someone else losing a priceless item they left in their vehicle: This is an open letter to those who leave price-less items in their vehicles and then are surprised when they get stolen. Your mom's ashes? Don't leave them in the car. Your locket that your grandmother bequeathed to you on her deathbed? Don't leave it in the car. Your father's war medals? Don't leave them in the car. Your laptop containing the only copy of your thesis? Don't leave it in the car. When you take to Facebook and tell us it was stolen, we feel badly for you but we also want to say, "Don't leave it in the car!"

• • •

Conversation with Bob:

Bob: "Do you still seek fame and fortune?"
Me: "Yes, but at my age I'll probably have to murder someone to gain fame. Actually, Just murdering someone wouldn't be enough; I'd have to become a serial killer like Dexter."
Bob: "You've given this some thought?" (worried look)
Me: "No. You asked if I still sought fame and I just said that time is running out on that dream and I'm running out of options. You have to admit, I'd certainly become famous if I was a serial killer."
Bob: "You worry me, Judy . . ."

• • •

During a trip to New York with my daughter: Walking home tonight from the outdoor theatre and we walk past the Trump Hotel. A horse and carriage clip clops its way up and parks in front. I see no one in the carriage except for a driver and a monkey. I say to Amy, "Look at that monkey," to which she replies, "That isn't a monkey, Mom, that's a little girl! With pigtails!" #lookedlikeamonkeytome

• • •

Some days I imagine my brain is a circus clown car filled with many tiny clowns. Some are hanging out the windows, some have their heads through the sunroof. There are angry clowns and happy clowns and sleepy clowns and sarcastic clowns. Yes . . . this is what my brain is like some days.

Pssst! I have a Phablet

• • •

I DID IT! I FINALLY did it! I switched from my Blackberry to a Samsung 'Phablet'. For years I've been mocked for my allegiance to my Blackberry – my resistance to switching to the touch screen so popular with the iPhone generation. It isn't because I don't love Apple products, because I do: I've owned three Mac computers and an iPad. The thing is, I was concerned that I'd sacrifice texting speed and efficiency if I abandoned my slide-out, QWERTY Blackberry keyboard. I'm only five feet tall but I have freakishly gargantuan fingertips and could envision myself desperately trying to tap out a quick message. Losing my ability to articulate with words that contain more than one syllable because texting anything longer than a "yup" or a "k" took too much time. As a Blackberry user, in a flash I could text Margaret Atwood-worthy diatribes to my Facebook status without a spelling or grammatical error! Do you know who invented texting shorthand? The original iPhone user! It was shorthand borne out of a combination of frustration and autocorrect. I call it the 'Bieber Effect' on society.

In the end, my Blackberry made the decision for me: The battery refused to keep a charge. Then I received a call from my phone plan provider to let me know I was eligible for a new phone. It was like a sign. It was time to let him/her/it go.

My new phone is a 'phablet' (a combination of phone and tablet). Imagine holding up your iPad Mini to answer a call and you'll get the picture. I call it my 'calculator' because it's the size of a calculator. In fact, I've been taking most of the calls on 'speakerphone' because I'm terrified of over-developing the muscles in my right arm. I know it sounds like I'm dissatisfied with my new purchase but, honestly, I'm not. My new phablet is pretty phabulous and, unlike the Blackberry, there are plenty of apps to keep me occupied. I now have embraced the magic of Instagram (I know, I know . . . I'm pretty late to *that* party) and have become 'that person' . . . the person who filters EVERY SINGLE PHOTO.

Upon the advice of my son, I went online and watched YouTube videos to help familiarize myself with all the bells and whistles on my new phone. (Speaking of whistles . . . I immediately disabled the irritating whistle ring tone on my new phone – YOU'RE WELCOME!) Thank heaven I've never made a sex video or taken inappropriate selfies using my phone, because chances are I would have mistakenly emailed them while I figured out which buttons to press. I would like to apologize in advance to anyone who received the blurry picture of my fully-clothed lap . . . or the shaky video showing me holding the phone up and saying, "Is this the right button?" as I squinted with my failing eyesight (that's another conversation for another day).

I 'consciously uncoupled' with my Blackberry, but that doesn't lessen the grief and loss I feel after saying goodbye to my trusted friend. I cling to the good times we had . . . the way it effortlessly allowed me to manage multiple email accounts on my phone at any one time. Some people wear a Canadian flag on their backpack, but all I had to do was clutch my Blackberry in my right hand as I went through passport control, apologizing that I was unable to download the newest app designed to expedite the trip through American Customs.

In a way I was a Luddite of the smartphone world, shying away from fancy applications. Being a Blackberry user was the equivalent of going to Disneyland but not getting the brightly-colored wristband that allowed access to all of the rides and exhibits. Riding in the teacup, while others screamed in excitement from the roller coaster.

No longer will I have to worry after watching a news program about Blackberry stock, wondering if one day my phone will cease to operate because of poor third-quarter sales.

As a wise woman once told me: "Sometimes relationships end." Goodbye my beloved Blackberry . . . until we meet again.

The Pursuit of Unhappiness

● ● ●

STANDING IN THE LINE-UP AT the local grocery store, I noticed a semi-quasi-friend behind me. She noticed me noticing her, so I felt compelled to smile and ask, "How are you today?"

"Wonderful, amazing, soooooooo busy, loving life!" she replied.

I smiled and nodded, turning away, thinking, "I call bullshit."

She had dark rings under her eyes, her hair was in a messy (not in a good way) ponytail and one toddler was repeatedly kicking the cart while the other was crying.

If she had bothered to ask me how I was doing, I would have felt forced to respond with something like, "Oh yes, me too! Soooooooooo busy. Life is great!" My phony, enthusiastic smile wouldn't reach my eyes.

Both of us would be lying.

We have to.

Apparently . . . *'Happiness'* is *in*.

If you don't believe me, take a look at your Facebook timeline. Filled with expressive adverbs and adjectives, photos of dogs doing funny things and videos with a punch line.

We live with FOMO – the Fear of Missing Out based on these exclamation points shared in a Facebook post.

That's okay. Don't get me wrong, no one wants to read a timeline filled with negative thoughts or headlines. We can read the news to get that.

But come on . . .

EVERYONE has a bad day now and then.

EVERYONE gets irritated by a spouse or a co-worker.

EVERYONE feels lousy from time to time.

Why is it suddenly taboo to be a wee bit unhappy?

Is it because our unhappiness cannot compare to the unhappiness that's blanketing the world? We believe that we'd be ostracized or judged if we dared admit that we're "having a bad day?"

When our emotions are segregated to 'likes' and 'happy faces' and funny emoticons, there seems to be no room for sadness. Our responses have come down to shorthand text belying how we actually feel.

For what it's worth, I believe this is dangerous. The over-dramatization of our emotions, both good and bad, leaves little room for unhappiness. Somewhere nestled between 'amazing' and 'horrible' is a little place called 'fairly okay, but could be better'.

We shouldn't be afraid to share our unhappiness or our less-than-ideal emotions.

Being sad, feeling blue or having a range of emotions that fall somewhere inside the overdramatic spectrum that our social media-crazed society has created is normal and we should be able to share that with family and friends.

So . . . the next time a friend asks you, "How are you doing?" try being honest. You might be surprised at the outcome.

11. Pain Management

. . .

The Accidental Brazilian

• • •

I HAVE NEVER BEEN TOO concerned with the 'nether region' of my body insofar as whether or not it is 'groomed' adequately for the occasion. Sure, I would give it a trim every now and then but it wasn't like I went all 'Edward Scissorhands'.

There was a time that my pubic hair resembled an illustration from a 1970 Sex Ed textbook. In fact, I didn't even know that personal grooming was a 'thing' until my sister looked at me wearing my swimsuit and said, "Maybe you should tuck that stuff in." I found myself taking a good look for the very first time and realized that she was right! I was probably wearing a larger panty just to accommodate the overgrowth.

I then began a program of pubic deforestation. Nothing excessive, but enough to avoid sidelong glances at the public pool and people speaking really slowly to me because they figured I was European.

My v-jay-jay could best be described as "recovering Amish." If a v-jay bonnet was available, I would have pinned one on.

As I grew older and got married, I tended to 'groom' more often. Shaved my legs and armpits, waxed my upper lip and continued to deforest my growth. This kind of upkeep was simply not sustainable. My nether region hair grew faster than bamboo! I began to regress and pretty soon you couldn't see the forest for the trees.

Years passed . . .

When I was 40ish my dear friend was diagnosed with breast cancer. It's an unbelievable feeling of helplessness when someone you care about is diagnosed with cancer. You can empathize all you want, but no one can completely relate unless it's them hooked up to an IV getting poisoned on purpose to kill the cancer cells. At a complete loss, but needing to contribute to the cause, a group of us decided that we would create a calendar and sell it to raise money for the chemotherapy department at our local hospital.

What would make our calendar stand out from all the other calendars flooding the market? Well . . . we would pose nude. Yup! We decided that we would take our clothes off and have someone take 'artful' photos of our nakedness. Because . . . didn't you know? Every soccer mom wants to hang a calendar with photos of naked women on their refrigerator.

It was a noble cause and one that ended up raising over thirty thousand dollars.

But let's back up and discuss my overgrowth situation and the fact that I had committed to posing nude for a calendar.

Some grooming was in order!

I made an appointment with a local esthetician who came highly recommended for her bikini waxing capabilities. My only caveat is that I could not know them personally and not travel in the same circles with them because I didn't want to run into them downtown and become embarrassed. I'm old-fashioned like that.

The morning of my bikini wax I had a hot, hot shower and carefully shaved my legs, after which I lathered my body down with scented lotion. I selected my nicest underwear and got dressed for my appointment. I even took an Advil prophylactically in anticipation of some tenderness and slight swelling at the wax site. It was like I was a fresh-faced hooker anticipating her first client!

Sitting in the waiting room I felt a sense of empowerment. Heck, I was going to let someone other than my gynecologist and husband[60] see me in my underwear and I was going to tame the lion down under! It was a big day.

I felt her presence before I heard her voice. She felt warm and serene – a calmness about her being. "Judy," she whispered, "please follow me."

---

60 And generally the lights are off and the room-darkening blinds are pulled down so technically he hasn't seen me in my underwear for many years.

She was beautiful, with raven-black hair and porcelain skin. Her footsteps made no noise as I followed her down the long corridor to the patchouli-scented room. A large, padded table sat crosswise in the space. It was covered with a fresh, crisp white sheet.

"Please, take your time getting disrobed," she said, and then left the room quietly.

I wasn't familiar with the protocol.

Do I take off everything? I mean, can I leave my shirt on? What about my socks? What about my underwear? Can she just tug the gusset to one side to access the wax area? Did I wear the nice underwear?

I did the best that I could. I left my shirt and underwear on, but took my socks off because it looked weird. I hopped up onto the table and waited.

Knock, knock, knock . . .

"Come in!" I said, loudly enough for her to hear through the closed door.

Quickly she came into the room and busied herself with organizing the wax strips.

"Okay now . . . before we begin you should probably take off your underwear."

I nodded and then, while staring at the ceiling, I slipped off my panties and tossed them onto where my jeans were crumpled on the chair beside the bed. The panties were rather large and they caught the air and fell just short of my jeans. Giving up and lying back, I continued to stare at the ceiling.

I was embarrassed and also felt a bit naughty. I couldn't look this beautiful woman in the eye while she was grooming me!

She commenced.

The pain was horrific but she went about it so quickly that I barely had time to flinch between wax strips. She was clearly an expert.

After only a few moments she said, "Would you like a particular pattern? A landing strip perhaps?"

We have to understand something. I don't even know how to order a fancy coffee at Starbucks using their jargon, so now I was completely lost. Landing strip?

"Take a look and let me know," she said.

I opened my eyes and sat up slightly. Looking down I could see that only a small patch remained of what was previously an overgrown mass of hair. The rest of it: gone!

I was well on my way to a Brazilian waxing!

Too embarrassed to admit that I'd only wanted a light pruning and not a complete deforestation, I said, "Take it all" and laid back to once again stare at the ceiling.

Knees were clasped and hugged to my chin, wax was applied and removed and this wisp of a girl with raven black hair and porcelain skin grabbed, pulled back and lifted my anatomy to access every hair follicle that she could access.

"Done!" she said quietly and set a bottle of water in my hand. "Just lie here for a while and take your time getting dressed. I'll meet you out in the lobby."

And lie there I did, the burning sensation of the wax removal now giving way to a swelling sensation. I looked down and the first thought that crossed my mind was 'a plucked chicken' and then I thought 'a hairless cat'. My pubis was bare and I looked like a twelve-year-old.

I dressed carefully, cold in places that I had never felt chilled before.

I was euphoric! I had a Brazilian!!! It was like I had a secret that only I knew about.

I called my friend. "I just got finished at the spa."

"How did it go?" she asked, knowing that I was a bit nervous going in.

"It went . . . all right," and then I laughed. "I GOT A BRAZILIAN! EVERYTHING IS GONE!" I screamed into the phone.

I explained to her what had occurred and that I had been too embarrassed to tell the esthetician that a mistake had been made and that I was only there for a bikini wax.

Fast forward a week and picture day had arrived! The swelling had gone away and I no longer looked like I required medical attention. I was finally feeling good about the new me and not that embarrassed about having others see me.

The photo shoot lasted all afternoon. We all drank wine and wore pink robes, laughing and feeling a sense of accomplishment. I ended up having two photos in the calendar: one of my back with my arms over my head and another of the underside of my breasts (the camerawoman actually took the photo while she laid on the floor looking up at my body).

It was an experience I'll never forget. For the first time in my life I felt comfortable in my own skin.

Fast forward a few weeks. I did have a follow up appointment to get my Brazilian wax job redone about six weeks later, but by the third week, I could not find a corner of a table sharp enough to relieve the itchiness I was suffering while the hair grew back.

I managed to make it to the sixth week and went to my appointment to get 'freshened up'. My esthetician had moved from the spa and was now operating out of her home so I went to her house for my appointment. By this time I was familiar with the routine and quickly disrobed and hopped up onto the treatment table assuming the position.[61] "Ding Dong", before she could begin the waxing, the doorbell rang and she had to leave the room. I laid back and waited, not realizing that the door to the treatment room had swung open and the esthetician's three- or four-year-old son had entered the room looking for his mother.

I was in no position to have a conversation. I managed to snap my knees together and sit up, pulling my shirt down as far as it could be pulled, trying to cover my girl parts from this child.

"Your mommy left the room, sweetheart" I said, trying to reassure the child that his mom had not gone far.

The answer satisfied him and he left the room as silently as he had entered, no doubt to look for his mom elsewhere.

That was my last Brazilian waxing appointment. I felt like it was a sign from the universe that I didn't need that type of exotic grooming. Hell . . . I don't even like wearing a high, tight pony tail – I like a bit of 'tousle' to my look – much more relaxed and less itchy!

---

61 The position being similar to the gynecological appointment position where you relax and let one knee rest against the wall.

Now Serving #19

● ● ●

THE TIP OF MY NOSE had almost touched the clear glass before the lazy electronic eye noticed I was there and triggered the door to open in front of me with a whoosh. Forgive me. A 'whoosh' indicates that it opened quickly and with purpose, whereas this door opened like a petulant teenager: only moving fast enough so that no one can say it didn't try.

The waiting area was quiet with the exception of a young couple at the counter chatting with the receptionist.

'Now serving #19' flashed above the desk and I quickly scanned the room looking for further instructions on how this 'going to the emergency department' thing worked. A sign attached to the desk said 'Take a number and wait for the number to be called' but for the life of me I couldn't find a number dispenser anywhere.

I felt a wee bit panicked. It had been years since I had needed to make an emergency room visit and the current protocol at reception was throwing me.

Do I sit? Do I stand?

The folks at the counter wrapped up their business and moved away with paperwork in hand and I hesitantly moved forward.

It was 8 p.m. and it was clearly the end of a very long day for the receptionist. Smiling, she asked, "Can I help you?"

Whew . . . looks like my lack of #20 in hand was not going to be an issue. I moved in close to the counter and handed her my medical card.

After fifteen-plus years, the information was still all the same; only the family doctor had changed. I nodded and said "yes" to most of her questions and then waited for a printout that would allow me to proceed through to emergency.

You can't go through to emergency without the paperwork. It's like trying to cross the border into or out of Russia or North Korea. "Paperwork please!" Your paperwork is your passport that entitles you to travel the road to recovery . . . or at least to a prescription for antibiotics.

Rounding the corner, I was struck with how busy it was. Uniformed police officers were milling around a bed in the far corner, the paramedics had just brought in an elderly man who was clearly confused and there was a 'screamer' in the bed closest to the waiting area. If you closed your eyes, it'd sound like you were standing at a rave or a rock concert.

I decided to sit outside the traditional waiting area, away from the coughing and crying, snuffling and sneezing.

I still had one hurdle before I could join the queue of patients waiting to be seen. I needed to WAIT BEHIND THE PARTITION until I was called forward to triage.

I capitalized that because I envision someone very authoritatively dictating that to someone: "We need a sign and that sign needs to be very clear! We can't have people wandering in willy-nilly! They need to WAIT BEHIND THE PARTITION!"

I know why they do this and I don't blame them. Signs aren't created for the majority of the people . . . those people who don't barge in but instead patiently wait their turn. No, signs are designed for those folks who feel an overwhelming sense of entitlement and who aren't familiar with the concept of waiting.

For those impatient people there are further reminders, stating that 'Verbal abuse, etc. will not be tolerated'.

Note to self: Tell someone that it might be important for the hospital to create an empathy map for the emergency room.

Before you even set foot inside the hustle and bustle you're reminded of how powerless you are in this situation.

After approximately forty-five minutes I'm finally next in line to be triaged. At this moment a women briskly walks in and stands right in front of the stop sign, and begins to huff and puff impatiently.

I say, "I'm next, and then (gesturing to the ten or so others sitting around me), these folks are next and then you." In other words, "Sit down, sweetie. I might be in pain but I will TAKE YOU OUT!"

The look on her face was priceless and after a little extra 'huff and puff' just for me, she found a solitary seat where she could settle in for the long haul.

"Who's next?" I heard from beyond the partition and I scrambled past the divider to the waiting nurse.

"What are you here for, sweetie?" she said with a smile as she began checking blood pressure, pulse and temperature.

"I have a rash and I think it might be shingles," I responded, moving my top slightly so she could see it clearly. My rash is prepared for this dog and pony show and looks angrier than it did when I left the house an hour ago.

"Oooohhh," she clearly winced. "How is your pain? If you were to tell me on a scale of one to ten, with ten being the worst pain you have ever felt, what would be the number?"

My competitive streak rears its ugly head and I know I can handle a lot of pain. "Oh, it's probably only a five. I can handle much worse," I responded with a laugh.

She smiled conspiratorially with me . . . that smile that says, "Thank goodness you aren't going to be a pain in the ass tonight with your whining and wailing."

We had the "do you have allergies?" conversation and the "what medications are you on?" conversation and then she told me to return to my seat and wait.

Once again I sat beyond the STOP HERE partition, distancing myself from the real 'sickos' and not really considering the fact that shingles is the chicken pox virus and probably more contagious than Asthma Girl or Diabetes Man who were both visiting the hospital that night.

Another hour passed with no one called back into the treatment area. It was difficult to tell who the medical professionals were . . . no one wore a white coat or a cap. The nurses were all wearing something different and one was even wearing something resembling a black track suit. The only consistency was the hospital credentials worn on lanyards or clipped onto a waistband.

I didn't even know which one was the doctor. There was one man who seemed to move from bed to bed, lingering long enough for me to assume he was providing some type of care. He had a very long, 'robust, unkempt' beard, not unlike what I imagine Jesus to have had, and therefore in my mind he was now known as 'Doctor J'.

I am a little disappointed with my analogy. He might have looked like Jesus but he didn't work as efficiently as I imagine Jesus would. I mean . . . no one had been treated yet and the waiting area was overflowing. At this point I would have appreciated some water turned into wine, simply to take the edge off.

I texted my husband. "The doctor on call looks like Jesus so you'd think he would have this healing thing down pat."

I text my mother. "The doctor looks like Jesus and I'm pretty sure there's a bird nesting in his beard."

No reason I couldn't be sick and be funny . . .

Unfortunately, my phone autocorrected that to read, "The doctor looks Jewish and I am pretty sure there is a bird nesting in his beer."

So my mom texts back, "Jewish? Beer?"

"No. I meant Jesus. He looks like Jesus and that should have typed beard, not beer," I tap back with a sigh.

Then I typed out to whomever was still online, "The strategy this evening is to take so long that we either leave or die."

Badump-bump (taps the mic . . . is this thing on?)

We had now entered hour three and still no movement from the waiting area, with the exception of two people who walked in from the Emergency Ambulance Bay and who were clearly bleeding.

Blood trumps strange rash. I'm okay with that.

Laughter erupted from the cramped waiting room and I was curious so I grabbed my things and relocated to where the party obviously was being held.

It was the television. Everyone was mesmerized by a show about domestic cats. The laughter was over a video of a hairless cat.

We made up an unlikely group of people: An elderly man and woman who'd been there since I arrived earlier and were clearly exhausted. The man kept squirming uncomfortably in his wheelchair while the wife busied herself crocheting a blanket. At this rate, she might finish it, I thought. A young woman held her flush-faced sleeping daughter in her arms. A man struggled to breathe; I could hear the wheezing from his chest.

And me . . . and my rash.

The wheezing man offered me his seat and I said, "No, I've been sitting for hours, thank you" and I leaned against the wall and resumed watching the cat program.

I heard some activity behind me. "Mr. X had a bowel movement" said a nurse to her counterpart behind the nursing station. "Someone needs to clean it up . . . Wait! Mr. X! Don't get up . . . we're coming to help you!" and they both ran past the curtain where Mr. X was laying.

Poor Mr. X . . .

Rubber-soled footsteps approached and we looked up to see a petite nurse wearing cheerful pink scrubs. We leaned forward excitedly. She held a pile of charts in her arms and began calling out our names. False alarm. She simply was checking in, re-assessing each of us, making sure that none of us were sicker than when we arrived.

Two people don't respond to her roll call. They were tired. They'd left. They were all behind me so it offered me no unexpected advantage.

"How would you rate your pain?" she asked me, referring to my chart.

My pain . . . my pain? I was so tired that I couldn't distinguish between pain and exhaustion. It had now been three-and-a-half hours of waiting and the time was nearing 11:30.

"I'd have to say it has grown to a seven," I said tiredly, but honestly I didn't know anymore. In the back of my mind I wondered if I said "fifteen" would it move me to the beginning of the imaginary, unmoving line?

The elderly man wanted to leave and said as much. "I want to go home but my wife insists that we stay."

The nurse was kind. She understood and shook her head as if to say, "I know it has been a long wait."

A prompt then appeared across the screen of the television. "This television will revert to standby mode shortly."

What does that mean? We all looked at each other and I said laughingly, "It will probably turn off."

And then it did. It turned off.

We all laughed. We were all in this together now and had bonded like survivors on an island. Wheezing Man stood up and reached behind the television to find the button to bring forth life to the screen.

The cat show was over and a new program began and someone said, "Hey, we've seen this already!" Oh my goodness! They've been waiting for so long that they're still here for the second airing of a program.

Wheezing Man began to change channels just as a new doctor comes forward and said, "Mr. S?" and scanned the room for a response. The elderly woman jumped up (yes . . . jumped) and tossed her crocheting into her handbag. With a deftness that belied her visual age, she began pushing her husband's chair toward the treatment room with the efficiency and control of a seasoned airport porter.

You didn't have to ask her twice.

I wondered where Doctor Jesus went? I hadn't seen him for hours.

I sat down and Wheezing Man leaned over and asked, "What are you here for?" – akin to an inmate asking the same question.

"Pulled muscle," I lied . . . embarrassed to admit I was there for a rash on my boobage.

The new doctor meant business and in fifteen minutes the waiting room was almost devoid of people, with the exception of me and one other.

"Judy?" he called and motioned me to the room with the door. It was 12:27 a.m. and I had now been there four-and-a-half hours.

"What seems to be the problem?" he said kindly and with interest.

I pulled my top down to reveal my rash and before I said, "I think I have shingles," he said, "You have shingles."

It was 12:29 a.m.

For the next three or four minutes he explained shingles and how they can affect a person. He also said I should have come in sooner, to which I laughed and said, "I was here this morning once but left because, hey . . . it was just a rash."

12:34 a.m. and I had been given a dose of anti-virals and had a prescription in my hand for more. The waiting room was empty and the television was showing an infomercial about some type of blender. I couldn't see where Doctor Jesus was . . . he might have gone home, perhaps he was overwhelmed with the sheer number of walking wounded tonight. Perhaps the bird in his beard needed to be fed. Who knows . . .?

Once home I stripped out of my clothing and washed my hands thoroughly, washing the hospital off of me. I took my four oddly-shaped anti-viral tablets and crawled into bed. It was now 1 a.m.

I was strangely proud of myself. I stayed there for four-and-a-half hours. I didn't get angry, I didn't give in to the frustration. Everyone was nice. Everyone was patient.

Some would say, "It is what it is" and that's exactly right. "It was what it was" and nothing I could have said or done would have changed it.

Being powerless can be powerful.

Hoof Beats

• • •

THERE IS A SAYING: "IF you hear hoof beats, think horses, not zebras."

We hear it most often when someone is referring to a medical diagnosis, meaning, "If there are two competing diagnoses, one being simple and logical and the other being exotic and rare . . . think simple (think horses).

I have a difficult time knowing when to apply this theory. I think horses when surrounded by zebras and vice-versa.

Thankfully Dr. Google was not invented when my kids were growing up because I would have been at the family doctor regularly stating things like, "My daughter has a rash, do you think it might be chikungunya? (a nasty viral infection transmitted by mosquitos, most often found in Africa and Asia)." I would see zebras EVERYWHERE!

Even doctors make this mistake. Once I visited an E.R. with an extremely damaged hand from a fall during roller derby practice (yes . . . roller derby). My fingers were twisted in all sorts of directions and I was giddy with shock. The doctor took a look and declared "Dislocation" and I happily walked out of the E.R. reassured that all he heard were hoofbeats of horses. Days later, when the hand was swollen to twice its size and the slightest touch to a fingertip would render me incapacitated with pain, I went to see my regular physician. The diagnosis following x-ray? Not just broken fingers, but a couple so badly shattered that the only way to heal them was to set them as best we could and hope for a successful outcome. Obviously the original Doc should have been thinking zebras . . . not horses.

That's a whole other story for another day.

Here's another example. When I was about eighteen years of age, I approached my parents with a medical mystery. My hands up to my wrists had become blue and I was concerned that I was suffering from heart failure (because . . . I was eighteen and that would be the logical thinking). My parents were worried, especially my father because he had suffered from heart issues and it was always top-of-mind for him. We were all seeing a thundering herd of zebras pounding the dry, scorched earth of the Serengeti. Thankfully, and before I could grab my car keys and race to the emergency room for what surely would become open-heart surgery, my uncle, who happened to be visiting, asked, "Are those new jeans?"

Of course they were new, unwashed jeans.

He then asked, "Have you placed your hands in the pockets today?"

Of course I had.

Here horsey, horsey!

Crisis averted.

So it's fairly obvious that I have difficulty distinguishing between the sounds of hoofbeats.

Case in point: My eyes are getting worse with age. In fact, if my body was deteriorating as quickly as my vision, I'd be getting one of those, 'I've fallen and I can't get up' buttons to wear.

The other day I was getting ready to leave for work and I dug into my purse to grab my five-dollar sunglasses. I put them on and immediately noticed something strange with my vision. One eye was darker and clouded while the other eye could see clearly. There was an obvious problem.

Amidst the din of the hoof beats I tried to concentrate enough to create a bit of a list: Had I suffered a stroke? (I smiled to make sure one side of my face has not lost the ability to function.) No, thankfully I didn't exhibit any of the stroke symptoms. My vision must be deteriorating at a rapid rate! How can one eye get so bad so quickly?

Sadness overwhelmed me and I left the office, resigned to the fact that my vision was on a slip and slide and careening quickly out of control.

I slipped into my vehicle, started my car and pressed on the brake while I placed my hand on the center console shifter, readying myself to place it into reverse. (Side note: Even though I'd convinced myself that I was going blind in one eye, I still felt that I was able to drive.) At this same moment I looked in the review mirror and began to laugh hysterically at my reflection.

My vision wasn't failing! I had simply lost one lens out of my five-dollar pair of sunglasses that I have a habit of tossing (sans case) into my purse. No wonder one eye was clear and the other cloudy and gray. The remaining lens was not only shading me from the bright sun, but it was also so filthy dirty that it was difficult to see through.

Tears sprung to my eyes (although with the broken sunglasses, I could only see tears in one eye). Relief washed over me as the sound of hoof beats faded away.

I thought to myself, "I'm not going blind! Thankfully, I'm just an idiot."

Home Remedies

• • •

HOME REMEDIES? NO, I'M NOT sharing a recipe for potato soup.

Apparently potatos can cure hemorrhoids. Onions can cure the flu. And . . . milk and bread can create a poultice to draw out the poison of a boil.

Yes.

What I said.

Apparently modern medicine has nothing on the treatments dreamt up by our parents.

I grew up with a dad full of . . . Well (cough) he was, and continues to be, full of many things (nice things, of course). He had personal knowledge/experience of many, many 'home cures' to experiment with at the drop of a cowboy hat. The second youngest in a family of ten children, he had probably seen his fair share of doctorin' over his lifetime. Mom was a city girl and Dad was a farm boy, and with that distinction came a different mindset borne of necessity. Mom would have gone to a doctor, whereas Dad would have tried a more 'local' cure first!

My mom, daughter of a school teacher and herself a school teacher (indication of attendance at a school of higher learning), might have been skeptical of these homespun medical miracles, but if she was, she never let on.

Some of them were absolutely bizarre: "Keep that piece of potato away from me!"

Some of them actually worked . . .

When I was a little girl I had a boil on my elbow that was angry red and swollen up to the point where I had a 'teet-like' appendage coming off my arm ('teet' is farm-speak for boob).

Honestly, it looked like an elbow nipple.

Family discussion ensued.

Go to the community nurse?

No.

Go the doctor?

Gah? That's sixty miles (yes miles; this was pre-metric system) away! No way!

Lance it?

Nope. As attractive as that sounded, the boil wasn't quite ready for a lancin'. Sweet heavens to Betsy, nothing got my family more excited than an opportunity to lance or pop something. This fascination has continued . . .

What if we make a milk and bread poultice?

Sure, let's give it a shot.

My memory is a bit fuzzy but I believe that warm milk and bread were mixed together to form a paste. The paste was then used to slowly build up a 'cast', layer upon layer, over the affected area.

When complete, the mixture hardened and, voila! I had a cast!

How very, very MacGyver of them!

Side note: Deep down I was thrilled! I had always wanted a cast but in those days I had cat-like reflexes and freakishly efficient motor skills and always seemed to land right side up. No broken bones for this gal.

I loved the cast, I forgot about my boil and I even put my arm in a sling.

Days passed . . .

The comforting scent of white bread and milk was now souring and I began to smell.

Correction. My *arm* began to smell.

A family meeting was quickly convened. It was evident that the cast needed to go and hopefully the boil (that everyone had forgotten about) would be gone.

Dad got out his jack-knife and proceeded to cut my hard, yellow, smelly, 'cast' off, which came off in one piece.

OH MY GAWD!

The smell was horrific!

My elbow was all shrivelled and stinky, but the elbow 'teet' was gone! The boil was gone!

It worked!

12. If I Only Had a Cape!

• • •

When Smoke Gets in Your Eyes

● ● ●

HAVE YOU EVER WATCHED NEWS coverage of a disaster and wondered, "What would I have done in the same situation?"

We always view ourselves as handling it so much better, reacting faster, being the grateful survivors interviewed in the documentary of the tragedy.

This is what we imagine:

Lady holding her small poodle, standing in front of what was her home, now destroyed by the tornado. "Mandy started whimpering even before the alarms began blaring. I grabbed my Bible and headed downstairs and locked us up in the bathroom." Holds dog up close to her face and kisses her on her open doggy mouth. "I owe my life to this puppy."

This is what really happens:

Situation #1: Sound asleep in a hotel room and I'm woken by the smoke alarm in the hallway outside my door. Do I:

(a) roll over and go back to sleep,
(b) get irritated by the smoke alarm and consider calling front desk to beg them to "turn it off,"
(c) hold perfectly still and listen to hear anyone else leaving their rooms because, duh, it's a smoke alarm, or,
(d) all of the above.

If you chose 'D', you'd be correct! After going back to sleep and waking up to *still* hearing the smoke alarm blaring, I did everything on the list. Yes . . . me! The girl who has a red sateen cape with the words 'Anxiety Girl' on the back and the ability to jump to conclusions in a single bound did not react properly to a true (well, it was actually a malfunctioning) smoke alarm emergency.

There would have been another winner of the Darwin Award had that smoke alarm been triggered due to an actual emergency.

Situation #2: Sitting on a beautiful Hawaiian beach watching the waves tumble to shore. All of a sudden we hear a horn continuously sounding in the distance, the whine reminiscent of something one would expect to hear during a ummmm . . . I don't know . . . a TSUNAMI? Do we:

(a) look from one to another and say, "Why is that horn thingy blaring?"
(b) look around at other beach-goers to assess their level of alarm, which might influence our course of action?
(c) stand up and look out into the ocean to see if there's a big wave rolling towards us?
(d) have a conversation about the fact that "they should really tell visitors what to do if that horn should blow?"
(e) finally pack up gear and make way slowly to our condo because we simply cannot relax with that horn blaring?
(f) all of the above?

Ding, ding, ding! If you chose 'F – all of the above', you'd be correct.

Apparently we (or maybe it's just me) suffer from the delusion that it *could never happen to us* and *this simply cannot be happening.* In both situations there was hesitation or blatant ignorance of the audible warning of impending doom.

Honestly . . . I disappoint myself.

I'm the person who has to check to see if she left the coffee pot on when she leaves the house. I'm the person who prints out maps of airports before traveling so she's familiar with the layout. I'm the person who has a Purell squeeze bottle in every vehicle and purse.

I am the 'Jump to Conclusion' girl!

Apparently I'm also the "It would never actually happen to me" girl and the "This cannot be real, there must be some mistake" girl.

A Dummy Runs Through It

• • •

I'M A KLUTZ AND MORE than a bit of a ditz. I know, I know . . . I appear intelligent, witty and generally delightful but that's just a façade for a much darker side. Although I gave up yoga[62] I have the innate ability to take my foot, wrap it around my head and insert it into my mouth. I know! Quite an accomplishment for someone with twenty-nine-inch legs!

I'm going to give you an example. A few years ago I entered my very first half-marathon race and was tremendously excited. Did I doubt that I might not complete it? Not at all. Did I think I would win or even finish in the top five hundred? Not bloody likely.

Now, race days are quite stressful. You usually don't get much sleep the night before as you're trying to hydrate, hydrate, hydrate and end up spending most of the evening in the bathroom. Worries about irritable bowels take precedence over most other thoughts.

Rising early the next morning, after a restless night, I walked to the park where the race was to begin. All I could think about was, "How many porta-potties are there?" and "Will the line to the porta-potties be long?" Strategically, I didn't want to place myself in the bathroom line-up near the front, but somewhere in the middle. I really didn't have to the urge to go yet and wanted to give myself plenty of worry time to fill my bladder.

It's amazing the folks that you meet in the bathroom lineup. There are tall people, short people, skinny people, fat people, elite athletes,

---

62 I lost a chakra in class and my third eye always insisted on challenging folks to a staring contest.

wheelchair athletes, older folks, younger folks . . . you name it. I found myself standing next to a nice-looking, forty-something man and we engaged in conversation. He looked extremely fit and confident and explained that he'd moved to the area to train for the prestigious Iron Man Competition. I explained that this was my first "Half Mary," and that I was excited, scared, intimidated, etc. He asked if I had a specific goal in mind for the race and this is where it got ugly. *DISCLAIMER: I was not . . . I repeat . . . I was NOT in my proper frame of mind. I can only assume that I was suffering from some type of pre-race metabolic imbalance and therefore not responsible for my verbal diarrhea.* I glanced back over the lineup of folks and responded with, "Ha! Well, it looks like I won't be last."

I know, I know . . . stupid, stupid Judy. I should have my butt kicked for even making a comment like that but, bear with me . . . I did get my comeuppance. I followed that comment by saying, "By the way, those are neat glasses. Is there a camera mounted on them or something?"

"No," he replied coolly, "I'm legally blind; that's a magnifier" and turned his back, dismissing me. Open mouth . . . insert running shoe!

To completely serve me right, at Kilometer 21 I was passed by an incredibly fit elderly man who was accompanied by his grandchildren holding a sign: *We love you, Grandpa. Happy 80th birthday.*

Making Lululemonade

• • •

EVERY YEAR I REVISIT MY bucket list. Visions of climbing Mt. Kilimanjaro or having a conversation with the Dalai Lama have flitted through my brain. Dare to dream, dare to dream. More realistic goals would be cleaning my fridge and sorting the socks basket.

Never, ever, did I imagine that the very first accomplishment would be 'flashing my booty'.

Let me explain.

After a busy Saturday morning running errands downtown, I returned home to relax with a cup of a coffee and a good book. Sitting in my living room, surrounded by my dogs and the reflection of the neighbor's Christmas lights in my window (I hadn't put my lights up yet), a feeling of love and gratitude washed over me. I mean . . . how much better can my life get?

It was at this point that something grabbed my attention. You know, when you see something that looks mostly right but a little bit wrong? Yes, that's what I was seeing.

Looking down at my 'yoga' pants (I'm calling them yoga pants because somehow wearing yoga pants in public is more socially acceptable than wearing sweatpants downtown) I noticed that the seams were on the outside. "Hmmmm . . . that's strange. I never noticed that before," I thought.

Standing up, I continued to examine my <cough> yoga pants . . .

Yikes! They *were* inside out! Red-faced, with no one other than my dogs to share my humiliation, I chuckled and quickly took them off to turn them right-side out. "Oh Judy, you silly girl," I muttered to myself.

I stopped. Yoga pants in hand, I looked down to see that the back of the pants were completely torn/missing (having been chewed up and eaten by my dog) with *very* little material left. I was mortified! I had just run errands downtown, with not only my pants on inside out, but my rear-end showing and NO ONE said anything!

A wave of cold and nausea washed over me and my mind raced back to that moment hours earlier when I'd fumbled around in the morning darkness, searching for my yoga pants that I had left on the floor . . . at the mercy of my dog, Riley, who loves to eat pants.

My next thought went to my choice of undergarment. What the heck did I decide to wear today? To be clear . . . this is an area of my wardrobe to which I pay little attention. As my friend Kenda queried later, "Were they festive or conservative?"

You'd think I would have felt a breeze . . . or a chill as I:

* Shopped at computer store
* Shopped at gift shop
* Stood in line at the bank
* Stood in line to get coffee at Tim Horton's
. . . With my arse/underpants showing.

Oh.My.Gawd.

Immediately I took to Facebook to share my activities. Partly because I thought it was super funny and partly because it was something Olivia Pope from *Scandal* (one of my favorite shows) would do to manage the crisis. She would say, "If we release the information, we control the message."

So I did.

I released the information. I even posted a picture of my pants.

Sixty Facebook comments later and I was reminded why I love social media. I have friends who not only share in my success but support me in my humiliation.

As one friend said to me, "Better ask Santa for new yoga pants . . . or a long jacket!"

When life hands you lululemons . . . make Lululemonade!

Anxiety Girl

• • •

"Judy, you have a tendency to embellish."

"Judy, you're a wee bit over-dramatic."

I know, I know. It's difficult to imagine, much less believe.

How about Anxiety Girl: Able to leap to the worst conclusion in a single bound. (Thank you to Jennifer for coming up with that one.)

I've requested a cape.

You may be asking yourself, "Hmmmmm . . . what prompted this declaration?"

Let me share.

A few weeks ago, while lounging in my favorite jammies and enjoying an early-morning coffee, I noticed an older gentleman walk slowly in front of my house.

I live in a cul-de-sac and many people like to stroll around the crescent because there's very little traffic. I noticed this man because I didn't recognize him as living near me and he was walking quite carefully, as if he might be recovering from something or perhaps rehabilitating from something.

I returned to my early-morning ritual of checking Facebook and watching funny cat videos, but still was aware of this 'stranger' in my neighborhood.

He slowly made his way to the corner of the grassy park and suddenly collapsed on the ground. He basically buckled at the knees and fell to the grass in slow motion. It was at this point that he appeared to be frantically grappling for something in his pocket. I imagined *and* assumed he was a rehabilitating heart patient who'd overdone it and was suffering angina. The frantic search must be for nitro (heart meds). In retrospect, I realize that he also could've been stung by a bee and was now trying to pull out his epi-pen before he suffered a deadly allergic reaction, but hey, things were moving pretty fast and my brain can only jump to one conclusion at a time.

Did I mention that I was in my favorite jammies? Yes? Well . . . did I mention that the 'jammies' were actually a nightie I've owned since 1985 that used to skim my knees but now barely covers the kibbles and bits. Did I mention that the nightie is so thin and threadbare that it leaves absolutely nothing to the imagination? It's basically cheesecloth with sleeves.

So I leaped from my chair, spilling coffee on my thin nightie, wrenched open the front door and ran across the front lawn yelling, "Are you all right?"

I was prepared to do CPR. Is it one breath and five compressions? Do they even do breaths anymore? Oh damn! Why did I channel-surf past that Dr. Oz special about heart attacks? Yes, *this* was all running through my mind in the few seconds that it took me to run across the lawn.

I was much closer now and even without my progressive lenses on I noticed that the (very much alive) gentleman had ceased flailing. He rolled over and leaned casually on one elbow, having retrieved his cell phone (not nitro) from his pocket and said, "I'm fine. I'm just waiting for my wife to pick me up."

Seriously?

Relieved that a potential life-altering crisis had been averted, I now realized that I was standing somewhat naked-like on the front lawn. The morning light was streaming through the thin nightie and it's at this point that I reminded myself to write 'purchase new razor' on my shopping list.

Sigh . . .

I am truly worthy of my labels. But, in my defense, people like me are placed on this earth for a reason. We might jump to the odd conclusion, tend to be over dramatic, but – darnit! – we're always ready.

Twerking for Dummies

• • •

LAST WEEK I 'DANCED LIKE no one was watching' and stubbed my toe so badly that it bled. You know, when you hit your foot against the corner of the wall and it separates the big toe from the toe beside it (the no-name President's Choice toe)? Well, that's what happened. No one was home and that infectious song *Happy*[63] was playing on the television. Jumping up, I began to dance around the living room, my two dogs (who were confused and thought I was having a seizure) were barking and darting in and around my legs. Sweat began to bead onto my forehead and I wondered, "Exactly how long *is* this song?" But still I continued to dance. Abandoning my fur-lined slippers, I began to move much like I imagine Beyoncé might move. My too-short, stained pajama pants with the ragged drawstring tied into a ball of knots floated about my body and I began to twirl like Stevie Nicks.

That's when it happened! Pain like the pain of a thousand child-births shot through my foot and I crumpled to the floor: barking dogs now panicked because they were *certain* I was seizing and probably were afraid they wouldn't get fed. Dizzy with the pain, I attempted to see if I'd truly injured myself. I saw blood. Not a lot of blood, not enough for a band-aid, but there was some blood. Wiggling my big toe and then the no-name toe beside it, I checked for broken bones and was relieved that they both moved freely. (Note to self: Make a pedicure appointment.)

What the hell was happening to me? I used to be agile like a very short, stout Ninja and now a simple Twerk attempt could be my demise?

---

63 You remember Happy, right? That catchy ear worm from 2014?

The previous week I tripped going 'up' a flight of stairs to an aircraft. Envision my laptop case on one shoulder, a purse that technically should count as a carry-on over the other shoulder, and carrying a suitcase I would try to coax into the overhead bin on the aircraft. Smiling, pleased that my flight was on schedule and we were boarding on time, I began to climb the stairs. On the fourth step I tripped and, because my arms were full, I pitched forward in slow motion, my chin coming to rest on the ledge below where the flight attendant was standing. Her non-reaction indicated to me that she'd seen this kind of thing happen before and she waited for me to struggle to my feet. I understand she was practicing a type of 'tough love' and that I needed to realize that perhaps I was loaded over my maximum GVW. I did get the impression that she might have been holding back a snort of laughter/a guffaw (her shoulders were shaking so she was either crying or laughing).

I managed to navigate the final steps successfully and find my seat, where I now had to put everything away. This is where the 'objects may be larger than they appear' thing happens. I tried to force my suitcase into the overhead bin. It *should* have fit; I did size it using the metal sizing device located in the boarding lounge. The flight attendant no longer looked cheerful and came up beside me. "Is it too large?" The look on her face was reminiscent of the look my sister Jessie would give me when she dared me to do something. I matched her steely look with one of my own and responded, "No, it will fit. I *know* it will". Determined, I huffed and pushed until finally it slid down into the bin. Embarrassed that I'd scuffed up the edge of the opening on the bin in what appeared to be a brand-new aircraft, I saw the flight attendant glaring and imagined she was thinking, "This is why we can't have nice things."

My point is . . . twice this month I've taken a tumble and I'm wondering if I need to enroll myself into one of those I've-Fallen-and-Can't-Get-Up programs. Is this a slow metamorphosis beginning to occur? Will my next order from Zappos be for Velcro-closing runners? Will I begin to wear my progressives ALL the time? Stay tuned . . .

13. The Bottom of My Purse

• • •

THIS CHAPTER IS LIKE WHAT *you will find in my purse at any given moment: tampons and hard candies that have escaped their wrapping, receipts so old that the ink has faded, and lipstick that I purchased on a whim[64] and tossed into my purse and then promptly forgot. Coin gathers in the lining of the fabric and my wallet bulges with loyalty cards that I can never find when it matters most. I suffer from wallet envy of those women who brandish a wallet where every card has a place and every place has a card. I imagine that is what their underwear drawer looks like. I imagine that they are KonMari[65] Method converts who fold their disposable grocery bags into tiny little triangles and line them up in a box.*

I guess what I am saying is that this chapter is a collection of oddly constructed ideas and thoughts – the misfits that have no other place.

---

64 Rarely do I wear lipstick.

65 Invented by Marie Kondo: a method of organizing known as the KonMari method, and consists of gathering together everything you own, one category at a time, and then keeping only those things which make you happy and then giving them a place.

My Bag of Fucks

• • •

********IF YOU ARE EASILY OFFENDED by profanity, then quit reading because, this story is loaded with FUCKS. Not just regular Fucks either: There are Daily Fucks, Flying Fucks, Fancy Fucks and Little Fucks.

Fuck a duck (that seemed to fit).

Consider yourself warned . . .

There is a science behind the number of Fucks each of us is able to give. We all have the potential to give all of our Fucks each and every day. We should be grateful that we have the freedom to give our Fucks for anything we wish. That's called democracy.

Sometimes I'm very lucky and 'My Fuck-Giveth Cup Runneth Over' and I need to stop and give thanks.

The point is, giving a Fuck isn't a bad thing. It means that you care. My goal is to illustrate that we do not all have endless Fucks to give and sometimes we have to prioritize our Fucks!

I keep a velvet bag that contains my daily Fuck-giving supply. I carry different Fucks with me each day, depending on my mood. If I'm short on sleep or not feeling well I will have a marked decrease in the number of Fucks available to me. I find that when I'm eating properly and exercising regularly I can carry a ton of Fucks with me with little exertion. Of course I might be a little bit manic sometimes and give all of my Fucks out at once, but those days are few and far between. I've learned to pace myself.

Of course I have Daily Fucks (DF) and they are given out every day. I have them set to auto-dispense so I don't have to worry about forgetting. These DFs are used for things like:

- My Family
- My Health
- Global Warming
- Homelessness
- Food Safety
- My Home
- World Peace
- Etc.

These powerful Daily Fucks simply roll over each day (they contain an 'evergreen' clause) and I don't have to pay much attention. They're like pre-authorized payments through your bank; just set it up once and forget about it.

I also carry some Little Fucks with me. These are for small, almost insignificant situations that warrant a Little Fuck-giving, but let's not go overboard. Things like helping a significant other find his/her keys . . . things like that.

I have a robust supply of Standard Fucks (SFs) and these, I find, go rather quickly if I'm not careful. Some days by noon I've already given out all of my SFs. I'm trying to allow others to perhaps pick up the slack by offering one of their Fucks from time to time. I mean . . . should I always be the first one to give a Fuck? Folks need to step up to the plate.

One of my favorite Fucks is my Flying Fuck! It's very powerful and the best part of having a supply of Flying Fucks is that they don't expire; you can carry them over until the next day. Honestly, I don't like to waste Flying Fucks on anything trivial. It's a big deal if I give a Flying Fuck. They are amazing.

Think about it. Wouldn't it be the best feeling ever to say, "Here! I give a Flying Fuck to you. Take it, cherish it, solve your problems with it."

Bam! And walk away with a Justin Bieber swagger or a Justin Trudeau verbal mic drop

Yes, Flying Fucks are amazing but they're becoming endangered. One day, probably in my lifetime, there will be no such thing as Flying Fucks. That's what happened to the Unicorns.

The number of Fucks you're capable of giving does not diminish with age. Young people get access to the same number of Fucks but they simply haven't been trained how to use them properly and they tend to narcissistically use them on themselves. Whereas the older we are, the more apt we are to sprinkle the world with Fucks. We know it is better to give a Fuck than to receive one.

Know the value of your Fucks and don't waste them! Liking someone's Facebook page or sharing their call to action does not qualify as giving a Fuck.

Don't live with regret. Give that Fuck even if you think they don't need it. If you hold back, thinking they'll be okay because everyone else will be showering them with Fucks, then next week maybe they'll be voted off the Island/Dancing With the Stars/American Idol . . . or maybe dead because you assumed everyone else was giving a Fuck. You could have done something, but you couldn't spare a Fuck – that's sad.

Don't hoard your Fucks, either. If you find that you go to bed each night with a surplus of Fucks remaining, you should re-evaluate your life a bit. You might be a sociopath.

Don't judge those folks who honestly tell you, "I gave out all my Fucks today. I have nothing left to give." There are folks who we all know who give and give and give. In fact, they give their own personal Fucks when they don't have to.

So print out this Fucking List and save it for the next time when someone says, "Hey! Don't you give a Fuck?" It will help explain why you're unable to rise to the occasion. You're simply out of Fucks to give!

Fabulous Fanny Packs!

● ● ●

LET'S DISCUSS FANNY PACKS. HONESTLY, they are a brilliant . . . yes, you heard/ read me . . . they are a BRILLIANT accessory that has received a bad review. Think about it. No purse on your shoulder, no chance of leaving it (and all your valuables) behind, no big wallet in your back pocket to hurt your hip, and it can almost double as a belt. Hands-free at all times, the wearer is able to text, carry a beverage or hold a camera with no fear of everything falling out on a carnival ride. Somewhere between its height of popularity in the 1980s and its short lifecycle into the 1990s, somehow, someone determined that a fanny pack was an embarrassing accessory.

Why?

Hmmmm. Perhaps because the normal position of the fanny pack is less than flattering. Worn in the back, it creates bulk to the derriere. Worn in the front, it creates bulk to the midriff. No one seems to wear them to the side.

The trick is to never overpack your fanny pack, lest you draw more attention to it. Most certainly stay away from plaid (which screams "I went to Scotland and all I bought was this fanny pack") and black pleather (which screams . . . well . . . it just screams). My friend Phyllis says that we could probably consider 'Burberry plaid' but everyone agrees that rhinestones are pushing it.

I vote to bring the fanny pack back and there are quite a few of you out there who agree with me! In fact, the reinvention of the fanny pack has been happening around us and <whispers> "you didn't even know it."

We live in a hands-free world! We have hands-free phones, hands-free cameras/computers (Google glass) and I don't know about you, but I can ride my bike with no hands. The world is ready for the triumphant return and universal embrace of the hands-free fanny pack!

The fanny pack conundrum comes from the design. The original, unflattering oval 'eye' shape (meant to hug the body), especially when grossly overpacked, creates the illusion of an unfortunate 'appendage' and prompts a doubletake by passersby.

Perhaps a simple redesign would be enough to bring the fanny pack back! Everything old becomes new again, doesn't it? Goodness gracious, if the peplum waist can come back not once, not twice, but three times . . . there's hope for the humble fanny pack.

Here are some of my redesign ideas:

The hands-free Diaper Dawg: A fanny pack designed to hold one diaper and a travel pack of wet wipes. Because, seriously . . . shouldn't our arms always be free to hug our children? <sniff>

The Business Buddy: A large, thin, square nylon pouch which can be worn towards the back, under a suit jacket. The perfect size for a single file folder full of important documents. Once again . . . hands are kept free to allow the wearer to play Farmville or Candy Crush on their smartphone. Think 'Murse' (man purse).

The Enviro-Pocket: Created out of renewable bamboo, the delightfully soft enviro-pocket can only be ordered in green. The 'pocket' is worn in the same manner as a traditional fanny pack; large enough to hold two reusable cloth grocery bags and a bike lock.

The Farmer Brown Bag: Constructed out of durable canvas (think Carhartt), the Farmer Brown Bag (FBB) is designed for durability and strength. Vaguely resembling a diving belt, the FBB belt sits comfortably around the front and sides of the wearer, leaving the back pouch free to rest against the seat of the tractor. The generous size will accommodate an extra-large lunch and a thermos for those long days during harvest.

The Snowbird Satchel: Designed specifically for our traveling snow-birds! Comes in a brightly colored tropical print, with oversized zipper pulls and comfort band construction. Large enough to hold passports, glasses and flip phone.

I could go on and on and on . . .

Karma

• • •

Karma came to visit today.
Running to the door, I was overcome with excitement.
You see . . . I had been waiting for Karma to arrive.
For years I had given of myself over and over again.
Everyone said, "Don't you worry, Karma will repay your kindness."
So I waited, and waited, and waited.
Today was the day!
Karma was at my door and I couldn't wait to see what she would bring
to me. "What goes around, comes around," everyone said.
It had finally come around!
Swinging open the door I greeted Karma!
Karma was standing there with empty arms.
Tears came to my eyes.
I had been a shoulder to lean on, a giver of sweat and hard work.
I had pounded nails, cooked meals, walked door-to-door.
Why was Karma at my door empty-handed?
Seeing my disappointment, Karma said, "I will repay your kindness if
you can tell me with a pure heart that you gave of yourself each and
every time with no expectation."
I could not tell a lie.
I *did* have an expectation of something.
I loved the rush of pleasure when I gave.
I loved to see smiles.
I loved to give happiness to others.
Shutting the door I realized . . . Karma *had* arrived.
Karma had been there each and every time I gave.

Let's Make a Deal

• • •

A 'Palliative Commencement' organizer?

The 'Afterlife" party planner?

An 'Exit' strategist?

All sound equally creepy, but I'm as certain as I'm sitting here drinking my Baileys and a splash of coffee that we will see a day where those services are for hire. Did I mention that I was a corporate event planner?

I can just see the website or advertisements now . . .

A video montage of a beautiful field of green grass with a voiceover by Morgan Freeman: "Death is difficult enough without having to worry about planning it as well. At *Field of Green* Death Planning, we help you design a death experience that your friends and family will remember forever!"

"Want to go out with a bang? We can arrange for an authentic eighteenth century canon explosion followed by a moving fireworks display. Note: Due to the extremely dry conditions affecting our region, fireworks are not available at this time."

"Our *Serenity Now* package is our most requested experience and, for a limited time, it's fifty per cent off! Note: We do request all payment in advance."

"Call 1-800-HEL-PYOU today to hear more about our remarkable offers."

"No detail is too small for our team at *Field of Green*. We even consult with our clients about mood lighting, as we feel it is an integral part of the exit strategy. Candles are an end-of-life mainstay and are included in every package at *Field of Green*. We are truly excited to now be able to offer locally crafted soy candles for a more sustainable experience."

"We also have introduced the *Bereavement Bundle*, which includes coloring books for children under twelve and a CD with a selection of inspirational music."

"Add one of the following to complete the bundle:

Push notifications: At time of death, our social media team will 'push' a notification via cell phone text to those family and friends you wish to advise of your passing. It can be a simple message or a beautifully crafted goodbye text. Our creative team will work with you to create something worth sharing.

Account cancellation: Upon your passing, we will cancel all email sub-scriptions and close online accounts.

Mortality Makeover: Our team of stylist and makeup professionals will ensure that your last day is your best day!

Call now for a free consultation. Please advise if you have any aller-gies that we should be sensitive to, or any religious requests you would like to include.

Remember: If death is coming to you, you most definitely should be coming to us!

Call today!"

Expectations

• • •

We're born with a positive disposition.
We come into the world with no concept of disappointment.
We're born with a sense of wonder.
Every single thing we experience is . . .
New
Fresh
Special
We haven't been hurt.
We want for nothing.
Everyone loves us and we love everyone.
Lullaby's and teddy bears and soft blankets . . .
Life is perfect.
We go to sleep knowing that today was great, but we know tomorrow
will even be better.
We don't know any different.
We're positively positive.
Until . . . we grow up and we aren't any longer.
What demons drive away our positivity and replace it
with cynicism and negativity?
They enter through our eyes and begin by distorting our outlook.
They enter our heart and plant seeds of sadness.
They take over our body and suck out our energy.
They spread throughout our brain and change our thinking.
We become Knowingly Negative.
We 'know' too much.
But, in reality, we don't know anything.
Every day has the potential to be better.
Every day we can choose to see the beauty.
Every day can be looked upon with gratitude.
It's up to us.
It's up to you.

Hello

• • •

My favorite movie is *Love Actually*.

I love the music, I love the actors and I love the message. (FYI: I'll watch anything that features Hugh Grant and Colin Firth.) The best part of this 2003 Christmas-themed romantic comedy? You might think it's near the end when the story lines converge, and the music builds and you find yourself smiling and crying at the same time. Don't get me wrong; that's a pretty wonderful part of the show. But my favorite scene, the scene that I loop on Youtube over and over again, well, that's the opening 'Heathrow Airport' scene.

I am a *Hello* junkie.

I love seeing 'hellos'. I love seeing the look on faces as they search the crowd, looking for that special person. There is a moment of worry (where even those with the most compromised posture will stand rod straight, necks extended), then they lock on with their eyes and their entire body relaxes and is overcome with joy and happiness. That split-second of calm, the moment of relaxation or reassurance where their shoulders sag almost imperceptibly, is something that I 'people watch' for.

It happens.

Every. Single. Time.

But you can't have the excitement and happiness of the hello without the gut-wrenching goodbye.

'Hellos' are littered with hand-painted 'Welcome Home' signs while 'goodbyes' suck every bit of air from the room.

'Hellos' are audible exhales while a 'goodbye' involves holding your breath.

'Hellos' can be loud and boisterous while 'goodbyes' are often silent.

I have an active imagination.

Just outside the boarding lounge I see a husband and wife sitting close to one another on an uncomfortable metal airport bench, thighs and shoulders touching, neither one saying a word. They're simply 'together' for these last few moments before she leaves. In my mind I wonder . . . how long will they be apart?

An adorable, elderly couple holding hands. I imagine the warmth in their grasp that is loving, familiar and simple; it's obvious that hand-holding is a daily occurrence. She might be thinking, "Will he be okay while I'm gone?" He's probably thinking, "I will miss her."

A mother and father clinging to the final moments with their university-bound son or daughter. A hug that says, "I can't bear to let you go."

The grandfather sitting with a grandchild on his lap, drinking in every drop of the moment because he knows that the next time they see one another, both will have changed.

And then the plane is gone and that moment is over and the excitement of the 'hello' begins to build, its momentum seemingly erasing the angst of the goodbye.

The next time you say goodbye to someone, take a second to imagine how beautiful the 'hello' will be, because you can't have one without the other.

14. Middle Management

• • •

Old Ugly Rose

• • •

ACTUALLY, IT'S REALLY CALLED 'OLD Country Rose' and it's my china pattern: A collection of Royal Albert china that fills (I'm not exaggerating) my china cabinet, displayed through glass shelves for everyone to see.

Like in a museum or something.

It was 1982 and I was graduating from high school. While other graduates opened envelopes full of money, my post-graduation gift opening was an endless parade of gold-rimmed china pieces, all belonging to the china pattern known as Old Country Rose. When the gift opening was over, I was surrounded by tissue paper and an incomplete set of bone china. Thankfully, my wedding two years later (yes . . . two years later . . . insert banjo music here) served as an invitation to finish off the collection. Every nineteen-year-old needs a twelve-piece setting of fine china . . .

It was thirty-plus years ago and at that time everyone collected china. We also had *Hope Chests* at the end of our beds. My hope chest was made from cedar and had been crafted by my grandfather. If I were to describe it to someone now, I'd say, "It was a coffin-like container with a hinged lid, where I deposited my hopes and dreams for the future." My hodgepodge collection of fine china found its way into my hope chest, nestled next to my blue Treasure Album and partially filled autograph booklets.

As an homage to my Auntie Evelyn, I had chosen the pattern called Old Country Rose. I hadn't considered what my tablescape might look like completely set with this china pattern. The result could best be described as 'busy'.

My collecting came to an end in 1986 when, upon my opening a box containing a red rose-adorned olive dish, my husband proclaimed proudly, "Well honey, that's the last piece that we can find of Old Country Rose! You have them all!"

Yes, I had every piece of Old Ugly Rose. I had serving bowls and cake knives and nappies. I had olive trays and butter dishes and gravy boats. I had both a tea and a coffee pot and two sets of salt and pepper shakers. I even had a tiny bell and a china shoe covered in the whimsical pattern.

I'm certain my family was disappointed that shopping for me was now going to become a little more difficult. They've been thinking, "Now what?" On the other hand, I was ecstatic! Squealing inside, I knew that the great china purchasing competition had now come to an end and I might actually receive a gift that I could wear . . . or like, or use.

Did you know that the only color of tablecloth that you can place under a twelve-piece setting of Old Ugly Rose is white? Anything with a pattern will disrupt that little bubble in your brain, causing vertigo and, finally, nausea. Did you also know that fine china cannot go into the dishwasher because it might become damaged? Yes, it screams "use me!"

What prompted this travel back in time to discuss china? When my daughter was planning her wedding there was much discussion about Bridal Registries and what the happy couple might need as they began their <cough> journey together. I insert the <cough> there because they had been together for about four years prior to the engagement and, between combining his household and hers, they had almost everything they require.

No, Amy doesn't collect china and I warned her against uttering any words that family and friends, desperate for wedding gift ideas, might cobble together and conclude that she collects something in particular. You say you like owls and pretty soon every cup and tea towel has a creepy owl on it. You indicate that you enjoy Starbucks flavored coffee and for the next five years you receive bottles of fancy syrups. You say you like a piece of china and . . . well, you get the drift.

Bridal registries serve an important purpose. I didn't have one. No . . . instead I received things like teeny, tiny little glasses used for serving an aperitif (the six I received were given to Amy as a child to use in her tea set). I also received many mismatched picture frames and one giant, framed Batik. Don't get me wrong, the Batik was spectacular but didn't quite fit into my *Early Canadian Garage Sale* decorating scheme. Neither did the hodgepodge of picture frames, but that didn't stop me from creating a feature wall out of them in our first home.

No, Amy didn't need any china for her wedding . . . because I'm going to give her mine.

You're welcome, Amy.

The Dish Thief

• • •

IF YOU WERE TO OPEN my kitchen cupboards and look at my dishes, you'd assume I was one of those 'eclectic' people who choose to live in a state of 'nothing matches'. My dishes are a hodge-podge of size, color and type. I have stoneware, earthenware, Corel, china and porcelain, and only one of each pattern.

Why? Why would a grown woman have a cupboard full of dishes resembling that of a college student?

Because . . . my name is Judy and I am a thief– a dish thief.

I steal dishes and everyone knows about it. It is our family's 'dirty little secret' that isn't so much a secret because they've taken to mocking me about my habit.

Let's be clear: I don't go into your home in the dead of night and steal crockery. No, I simply will accept food in said crockery and never return it.

Does that still make me a thief? Or does it simply make me lazy?

Like I said, my family recognizes this trait in me and have taken steps to cope with my little problem. Mom has taken to providing leftovers to me in plastic Ziplock bags and my sister will snatch her dish off of the table as soon as we serve dessert, choosing to take it home without it being washed.

"Oh Jess, just leave it. I'll wash it and return to you," I'd say sweetly.

Jessie would snort in laughter and place the dish by her shoes and purse so she wouldn't forget it (and I wouldn't *accidentally* place it in my cupboard).

My family makes a point of 'making a point' of returning things.

The other day I was at my mom's and I could see that she'd set out the little chair I'd loaned her when she watched grandbaby Dylan. Inside the chair was a tea towel that looked freshly washed (and probably ironed . . . my mom loves to iron).

Mom: "Do you see your towel? The one I washed and put in Dylan's chair for you to take home?" (What I heard in my guilty conscience: *"Because I return things no matter how small or insignificant, unlike someone I know."*)

She might as well have said, "Oh yes, here's a little sticker that stuck to my pants when I was at your house the other day. I didn't want to keep it because it might be important and I return things. I'm a thing returner. I don't keep things."

I rolled my eyes and laughed. "I get it, Mom. I'm not good at returning things."

FYI - I don't simply steal dishes. I steal books, too!

When the children were little we would walk or ride our bikes to the library and take out books for the week. One day my card didn't work (dramatization).

You see, I hadn't returned all the books from previous week(s) and apparently they wanted them *all* back, not just a few.

The trips to the library ended until I could find that damn book! I thought librarians were peace-loving individuals but they take their books *very* seriously and if you don't return them . . .

That was the year I considered myself a 'Patron of the Library' because of the fines and late fees.

I haven't been to the library in years. I'm scared that there's a picture of me as a screensaver that says, 'DO NOT LEND HER A BOOK'.

My daughter is also a 'non-returner' and I'm sad that out of all the wonderful traits she could have inherited from me (come on . . . I have *some* wonderful traits), instead she inherited the 'Me no give stuff back' gene.

Both of us have become very nonchalant about it and a wee bit defensive. I mean . . . don't lend us stuff that you want returned. Don't give us your favorite stoneware dish full of lasagna and then be surprised when you see it gracing our table weeks later when we invite *you* for supper. Don't loan us your favorite book with the inscription from the author because you should know better and YOU ARE NEVER GETTING IT BACK!

I've come up with an idea to clear my conscience of my thievery.

When I die, I want my family to take every dish out of my cupboard and every book off of the bookshelf and take it to the funeral. When someone comes up to weep over my casket, I invite them to also look through the myriad of books and kitchenware and claim their plate, bowl, and covered dish or signed first edition.

Then I will rest easy.

Job Interviews for Dummies

• • •

"WELL . . . I CERTAINLY WOULDN'T SKI – I *hate* skiing." I leaned back into my chair, smiling confidently.

That was the idiotic answer I gave during a recent job interview and I'm still shaking my head with the ridiculousness of my answer in response to, "What would you never do?"

I believe it was question number fourteen out of an endless list of questions and my mind was grappling at the reasoning behind the five words. What? What would I never do? What??

So they rephrased and said, "What might you never do at work or even in your home life?" The interviewers had leaned in towards me, their bodies turning in their chairs, their stares and wooden smiles making me nervous.

"Yeah . . . ummm . . . well, I definitely wouldn't ski. Not downhill ski anyway, because I have cross-country skied and I wouldn't rule that out as a future activity except the boots hurt my ankles and it probably is because I have no core strength so I'm constantly fighting to balance and then my legs hurt radiating to my ankles." I was rambling and I knew I was rambling but that's what I do when I get nervous . . . I ramble.

The scratching sound of the pencil-lead on their paper seemed to go on forever. What were they writing?

In retrospect, they were probably writing, "Ask follow up question about past history of head injuries."

I didn't know it at the time but that answer quite possibly had removed all doubt from their minds that I was *not* a good fit for their organization.

No, not because they take ski trips as a team-building opportunity, but because I realized how stupid my answer was hours later when I debriefed with my husband.

"How was the interview?" he asked

"I think it went well, but they did ask some weird questions."

"What kind of weird questions?"

"Well, they asked me what I would never do and I thought that was really strange."

Bob turned to me and shook his head. "That's not a strange question. There are lots of things you would never do: lie, cheat, steal, etc. Right? What did you say?"

Confused, I shook my head. "What?"

"Well of course that question was designed to gauge your moral compass. Don't tell me you didn't figure that out?" Now Bob was laughing in that nervous way he laughs when he suspects that I've done something epically stupid.

Frustrated, I burst out with, "Well damnit! If they wanted me to answer it that way why didn't they ask it like that?"

"They *did* ask it that way! You simply didn't figure it out! What did you tell them?"

I muttered quietly, "I said I wouldn't ski."

"What was that? You have to speak louder and move your hand from your face so I can hear you better".

Sigh. "I said I would most certainly not ski".

"HAHAHAHAHAHAHAHA." Bob was laughing and snorting and pointing at me, all at the same time.

"You said what? HAHAHAHA! You said you wouldn't *ski*?"

"Don't laugh at me! I didn't understand the question and it's true! I won't downhill ski; my knees are bad."

At this point even the dogs were looking sympathetically towards me, almost as if to say, "For a smart person, you sure are dumb."

"Oh Judy . . . what did they say when you said that?"

"They just smiled and kept writing. There were so many questions and I didn't have a copy to look at which I should have probably asked for before we began!" Now I was whining and making excuses for my lapse in comprehension.

Thinking that perhaps Bob was wrong, I asked my mom the same question, to which she responded, "That question makes sense. How did you answer it?"

Now I had to admit my folly and Mom laughed and laughed.

"Oh, Judy."

It didn't come as a big surprise when I received the "Dear Judy, We regret to inform you . . . yada yada . . . you were unsuccessful . . . yada yada. We will keep resume on file . . . etc." letter.

Sad but understanding of the outcome, I got a pep talk from my friend who said, "Don't worry Judy. Perhaps they were looking for someone who enjoyed skiing."

Long Capes and Leggings

• • •

MY RESPONSE TO THE RETURN of the damn cape for anyone but Supergirl!

It's a cape, it's a wrap, it's a shrug!
Said to keep the wearer comfy and snug
The heavy yawn of material with no true form
Draped across shoulders to keep you warm
Touching the hips at an unflattering spot
A short girl's nightmare, one in which I have been caught
The pressure I feel to join this trend
Will the cacophony of peer pressure never end?
I have donned leggings and jeggings paired with long denim shirts
Worn high boots with buckles under a long flowing skirt
None of these look right or make me feel good
But I'm only fifty years old and if fashionable I should
Toss a cape overtop with fringes that hang
Disproportionately long in reference to frame
I become a fat Lilliputian with a teeny tiny head
A look that screams out, "I wish I was naked instead!"
But society dictates that I try to make nice
With these looks that are horrid and expensive in price
So I stick to dark colors and pair with large glasses
Because long capes and leggings make some of us (me)
look like fat asses!

Five Shades of Grey

• • •

DISCLAIMER: I HAVE RECEIVED PERMISSION from my daughter to publicly mock her. Her response to my request? "No problem, Mom . . . so pleased that I've provided adequate fodder."

My otherwise fairly reasonable, emotionally stable eldest offspring became a 'Bride to Be' in 2014 and this is the story about how she lost it - Oh, she fought a courageous battle, but at the intersection of picking the perfect font and tulle versus taffeta, she lost her mind.

During the nine months of planning she became a conundrum, wrapped in Dupioni silk and mini-lights, encased in fondant and sprinkled with glitter.

Da Dum (envision the musical intro from Law and Order) – this is her story . . .

"Mom, I don't know what's happened to me," she whispers into the phone to me late at night. I hear a rustling of pages and I know she has that damn bridal binder open on her lap again.

"Honey, just put the book down now. It's late. Everything (including the invitation font she's currently agonizing over) will look different in the morning." Then I try to make a funny by singing, a-la Doris Day, "Que Sans Serif, Seriiiiif, whatever will be, will beeeeee."

"Moooooooooooom! Don't make fun of me," she says, laughing, knowing that my gentle ribbing comes from a place of love (and sanity).

When I got married, the only real concern was, "Do we have enough tinfoil to cover cardboard letters to create our names and place high on the Legion Hall wall behind the head table?" In fact, my mother planned the entire thing and I just showed up.

Nowadays there's so much pressure for these young brides.

From the time Amy was a young teenager dreaming of her Prince Charming we've spent every long road trip planning an imaginary wedding. We've planned weddings with a Parisian theme complete with gold, pink and glitter, and we've planned country theme weddings covered in red and white checked gingham. We've pored over wedding magazines and watched every episode of *Say Yes to the Dress*.

Unfortunately, no one says anything about the indecisiveness that creeps in and overtakes the bride to be. Before she was engaged, Amy could 'Lean In' and make decisions with Sheryl Sandberg-like confidence. After the engagement, decisions were no longer easy . . .

Here's an example.

Before engagement:

Judy: "Amy, have you ever wondered what your bridesmaids would wear?"

Amy (taking a sip from her kale, cucumber and acai berry post-yoga workout shake): "You know, Mom, I believe everyone is an individual, you know? Like, it's important for them to be individuals and express that individuality, not put a label on it. In the end it's about them just being there by my side, right?"

After engagement:

Judy: "Amy, what are your bridesmaids going to wear?"

Amy (drinking her third espresso of the morning and blinking profusely): "They're going to be grey, but not just any grey. I want them to be the same grey as that Siberian husky dog I posted on my Pinterest page and I want them to be stretch taffeta or silk."

Pinterest . . . that old chestnut. Every bride to be has a Pinterest page filled with twenty different tablescape pictures and fifteen different lists and DIY projects. No wonder our young brides are losing their minds!

Back in the day, there was a simple recipe for wedding planning. Now we agonize over jelly jars and burlap and hope that it is 'pin worthy'.

Sigh . . .

13. When the Ninja Becomes an Alchemist

• • •

My Colorful World

• • •

AT ABOUT THE AGE OF five, children are placed in a classroom with Crayola wax crayons and poorly photocopied pages of a cornucopia or pumpkin and are told to celebrate the season of Thanksgiving by coloring! These same pages are sent home to adorn fridges across the land!

This is our first experience with our 'creative' side. Common sense says the pumpkin should be orange and the stem should be brownish green. The leaves decorating the cornucopia should be autumn blushes and the corn should look freshly harvested; the turkey should be brown and have a glossy finish.

Most very young school children are armed with flat boxes of wax crayons containing limited color choices: only one green shade, only one red, etc. The completed artwork looks similar; most children have difficulty staying within those darn lines.

The years go by and the artwork becomes more refined. There are those kids who have been lucky enough to be supplied with those jumbo boxes of wax crayons (you know . . . the ones where there are four rows of crayons lined up and placed according to shade). Two rows of little wax soldiers standing in the orchestra pit of the box and two rows standing above in the mezzanine. Some of these boxes had SHARPENERS built in! Oh.My.Gawd . . .

The colored pages decorating the walls of the classroom begin to vary: some by children who still struggled to remain within the lines; others by those who were unable to truly express themselves with a box of only twenty-four crayons and the colors contained therein; and finally, ones by those who took advantage of their jumbo box of waxy goodness and freely 'expressed themselves'. These are the same kids who were able to color Mrs. Claus using the 'skin' tone crayon, whereas the rest of us tinted Mrs. Claus' skin to resemble someone suffering with a biliary blockage.

The divide begins.

At approximately Grade Four the divide becomes a chasm. Enter . . . pencil crayons! Pencil cases containing sharpened pencils of beautiful pure color in every shade imaginable.

This is like graduating from sanitary napkins to tampons. There's no going back to wax crayons now!

Grade Four social studies involves the task of coloring and labeling a world map. The sharp point of the new pencil crayons allows the child to create something quite beautiful. But remember, you have to color inside the lines because you'd literally be invading another country with color!

I hated these maps.

Not only did it take an inordinate amount of time and required a vast array of tints and hues to label everything properly, there were those creative types who insisted on coloring their maps with enough hand pressure to create a 'glossy' look to their masterpiece. Pre-computer, these maps resembled something printed from a laser printer.

How do you decide on the color for each country? I mean, in some instances the outlines are so small on the map that it's difficult to distinguish one from the other. You have to, though. You have to choose shades that are different enough so that you can differentiate between smaller countries like Senegal and Mauritania. If you don't, your teacher might assume that you don't know the difference between Senegal and Mauritania!

Questions creep in . . . can you use a color more than once on the map?

So.Much.Pressure.

Coloring should be joyful and relaxing. Think about it! You're creating something completely different than anyone else. No one would choose the same color palette; no one would use the same hand pressure as they applied the graphite pigment to the page.

After my school years ended, I abandoned coloring. Even as a young mom, I never colored with my children. Coloring seemed so silly and part of my brain recalled how inadequate I felt handing in my map of the world or some other artwork.

Recently I purchased an adult coloring book. No, it isn't porn. It's a coloring book filled with pictures an adult might like. There are no Dora the Explorer outlines or pictures of Minions; instead there are these 'mandalas', intricate shapes and outlines that are challenging.

It's the world map all over again.

So many small outlines within the picture . . . the stress begins to build.

My pencil crayons are now finely-tipped markers with an endless spectrum of color at my disposal – and yet I begin to stress.

This picture is going to take FOREVER. It reminds me of sewing.

Can I let go of my younger self and my angst and begin to relax as I color? Can I proudly post my completed picture on the fridge beside the new photo of my grandchild? "Grandma can color!"

What does hubby think when he comes home from work and the dining room table is covered with half-completed pictures; markers and pencil crayons strewn around?

The answers are "Yes I can" and "Who cares?" Yes I can proudly post my crayon art and who cares what anyone thinks about how I'm spending my time?

I'm grown up now and it doesn't matter what colors I use or how many times I stray outside the lines. I color because it makes me happy.

Pucker up and blow!

• • •

"JUST PUCKER UP AND BLOW!"

Oh Jiminy Cricket . . . it isn't that easy! I remember when I *finally* learned how to whistle. There was tongue placement and mouth shape and the question of 'do I breathe in or out?' before any sound came forth.

I loved it when my dad whistled. He whistled when he worked, he whistled when he played the guitar or banjo, he whistled when there was an absence of sound in the room.

It was beautiful.

"Can you teach me, Dad? Can you?"

Patience was, and still is, not a virtue of my father, so thankfully I catch on very quickly when learning something new. It wasn't long before I could whistle my favorite Donny Osmond songs or music from the new Frankie Valli and the Four Seasons album. In particular, *Sherry Baby* sounded amazing when whistled.

My ability to whistle meant that I could take my music anywhere and play it anytime. I didn't know it back then but whistling was like having my very own iPod!

As I grew up, I continued to whistle.

Working in a government office, sharing my 'area' with another clerk, I whistled until she begged me to stop. I guess 'begging' isn't the correct word, but she did bring it up on numerous occasions until I became very self-conscious and tried to refrain while at work.

By then it had developed into a habit. I whistled without realizing it and the results were not always music to the ears of those around me.

I didn't whistle songs, per se, but rather I whistled snippets of songs. Imagine hearing *Ava Maria,* turn into *Sail Away,* then transition to *I Will Always Love You.* Confusing . . . right?

These days I rarely whistle. I'm not certain why I took respite from this habit. Perhaps it was my feeling of self-consciousness after many someone's made mention of my musicality, or lack thereof. It's sad that I allowed the opinions of others to keep me from doing something that I clearly loved. As I write this, I'm trying to whistle and my mouth is tiring quickly. My whistle 'muscles' have shortened and grown stiff with lack of use.

Damnit! I *will* begin whistling once more! I'm gonna whistle in the car, whistle in the shower and sometimes I might whistle while I work! And no one, I mean no one, is going to stop me!

There is music in my head that only a whistle can play . . .

The Real Wives of Northeastern BC

• • •

I HAVE A CONFESSION.

Here goes: Hello, my name is Judy and I'm a sucker for a man in uniform. Just not the traditional uniform.

Nope, I'm in love with a man who wears bright blue and yellow, flame-retardant Nomex coveralls.

You know what I mean, the ones with the lingering scent of condensate or some other smelly substance clinging to the material.

Believe me, there's no detergent that completely removes that smell. Even freshly laundered, the coveralls have a faint odor of Tide and something from the Periodic Table of Elements.

There are no shiny buttons or highly-polished footwear. No, this untraditional uniform consists of coveralls, hardhats and muddy boots.

Hearing protection dangles from plastic strings, and when it's not in use it rests against the white embroidered name badge that has been picked with a sharp jackknife to shorten the name.

You know what I mean: Robert becomes Rob, Matthew becomes Matt, Richard becomes Rich.

Hardhats are adorned with stickers and sometimes a nickname is scribbled across the short brim.

Although not in the military, my hubby and others just like him respond to emergencies and call-outs in military fashion.

A phone conversation with the alarm service in the middle of the night is barely completed and they're out of bed and making their way to work.

It doesn't matter if it has snowed all night or the ice fog is so thick from cold that they can barely see the highway. No! They get up and go to work.

I don't get up with him when he has a call-out. Because why should both of us be tired? I'm a horrible wife, right?

In the morning I *do* look in the fridge to see if he grabbed his lunch – or had a chance to make a pot of coffee before he left.

At first glance, the crumbs and dishes littering the countertop imply that he managed to quickly make a ham sandwich to take with him. But then I realize that I simply forgot to clean the kitchen last night.

He probably lined up at Tim Horton's with a steady stream of other sleep-deprived workers, grabbing a double-double and a breakfast sandwich. It's gonna be a long day for him.

What on earth did we do before there were 24-hour drive-thrus? Anyway . . .

I've always wondered why there are some people who insist on identifying those in the blue and yellow oilfield worker uniform as 'rig pigs' or 'oilfield trash'.

You know, my dad, my husband and my son aren't trash and my friend and neighbor isn't a rig pig!

I know, I know . . . sometimes we see them come into a restaurant with their muddy boots and think, "How dare they!"

And they probably considered that very same thing as they backed into their parking space.

They thought about taking their boots off at the door, but then remembered that they'd just finished working a fourteen-hour shift and that the mud was the least of their worries.

Instead, they chose a table near the door and left a large tip because they felt badly about making a mess.

I guess my point this morning is to ask why we generalize the oilfield worker industry with labels like TRASH.

Every industry has the good, the bad and the ugly.

Take an empathy walk in that blue and yellow oilfield uniform and let me know how it felt.

How did it feel celebrating Christmas a week later because you had to work?

How did it feel working all night when you had a terrible cold?

How did it feel missing your son's or daughter's first hockey game?

Has your opinion changed? Because that *is* the normal life of an oilfield contractor. That was our life.

If This Table Could Talk

• • •

IT DAWNED ON ME RECENTLY, as we gathered at my mom and dad's to dine on the final, final Christmas leftovers (gravy is a magical thing and can transform anything into a casserole): We had been sitting around that same dining room table for a very long time!

The pedestal table, created out of solid elmwood (that's what Mom said when I asked her) remains in beautiful shape. The table, purchased in about 1980 when we moved to Dawson Creek, came with six chairs and two table leafs. For special occasions, my sister would go to one end and I to the other and tug gently; the table would open up like a giant chasm to be filled by one or both table leafs. One leaf meant Grandma and Grandpa were coming to dinner, two leafs meant that something special was being celebrated.

If only that table could talk . . .

That beautiful elmwood table has been a silent witness to uncontrollable laughter when the entire family has remained after a meal to share stories or play games. The surface has been moistened with tears during particularly emotional conversations.

That table has felt the soft hands of my grandparents and the touch of my pregnant belly. That same table has been the drum for a toddler holding a wooden spoon.

That table has been covered with high school textbooks and piled high with wedding crafts. It has been a sewing table, a baking table and a gift-wrapping station. It has borne witness to the occasional over-share and has also been the keeper of secrets.

The table surface is remarkably beautiful, but has not escaped its tenure with our family completely unscathed. It reminds me of a wall in a home that was used to measure the children as they grew, a nick or an indentation that boasted a date and an age.

As our family grew so did the table. Six, then eight, then ten and now that table cannot hold all of us at once – even with both extensions inserted. At first, a smaller card table was added to contain the over-flow: The 'Children's Table' which held Amy, Erin, Tayler and Matthew. This recent Christmas, two long tables were added to the configuration, the resulting set-up looking like a Tetris game. Highchairs and stacking stools peppered the landscape.

The large pedestal table remained the central fixture, covered and protected by a thick tablecloth, laden with china from the china cabinet and cutlery from the felt-lined box.

After dinner, as everyone cleared dishes, put food away and cleaned the kitchen, the tables were disassembled. The two long temporary tables were collapsed and put away, the stacking stools stacked one on top of the other and finally, the two leafs in the elmwood table were removed and the tablecloth tossed into the washing machine. Freshly washed, the table gleamed, almost as if it was smiling and thinking, "My family is near. All is right with the world."

Camp Grup[66]

• • •

GOSH, I MISS SUMMER CAMP . . .

I mean, I don't miss the bugs, or the threat of bears, or using an outhouse, or the fact that it was REALLY DARK AT NIGHT, and not having a night-light was terrifying . . . but I do miss going to summer camp.

I miss the romantic side of summer camp: canoeing at twilight and hearing a loon call, hiking while singing "Faaather Abraham had seven sons sir, had seven sons sir, had Father Abraham . . ." and foraging for feathers, rocks and flora to glue onto a paper plate to prove that arts and crafts were actually included in the fee.

I miss meeting others from across (then Alberta) and getting them to sign my autograph book. Did you have an autograph book? I had one that was ruby red and gold, embossed with the word *Autograph* on the front cover. The book was designed to lie flat when opened, so that the celebrity (or newfound friend) could write something witty and include their name, phone number and address.

It was the retro version of Facebook. Instead of writing on my 'wall', new friends could write in my autograph book.

Oh, I miss summer camp.

Why aren't there more summer camps for grown-ups? It would be easy to facilitate, require only some minor tweaking to make it work:

---

66 Grup is the contraction of gr(own)up. Don't worry . . . I had to look it up, too.

- Cabins versus tents
- Margaritas versus Kool-Aid
- Showers with unlimited hot water
- No bed time, no wake-up call

Everything else could remain the same. Camp Counselors (former Life Coaches) would schedule our days to include crafts, singalongs, drama class, watersports, and probably 'Facebook Hour' (a dedicated hour where we could update our Facebook status and upload our Instagram photos).

I see friends posting pictures of their children heading off to summer camp and I feel nostalgic. I have fallen into that 'old person' memory chasm by either remembering my summer camps past as very, very good – or very, very bad.

I fail to remember that a black bear shredded our wall tent (with us inside), or that they set up a bear trap outside the food building. It was a big culvert thing that failed to capture anything except our imaginations.

I fail to remember that when our Greyhound bus had a layover in Edmonton en route to Hinton, the girl I was traveling with stole something from a store and I spent the next few hours desperately wanting to call my mother and 'fess up' (rat on her). I was convinced that she would turn me to her life of crime . . . a real-life Thelma and Louise.

No, I only remember the good times. The laughter as we tumbled out of the heavy canoe into the freezing, glacier lake. The scary stories around the campfire that involved something bloody or ghostly.

Our camp counselors would reinforce the importance of respecting nature, respecting our environment.

The final day of camp would bring tears and clinging hugs and comments like, "You are my best friend forever" or "I promise to write you when I get home."

The counselors would wave enthusiastically as the buses turned the corner out of sight. Like Disneyland characters, they kept up the smiling camp counselor façade until we were gone, at which time their smiles probably vanished and cigarettes and cold beer suddenly appeared in hand.

Oh cynical me . . .

I miss summer camp.

Silence is Acceptance

• • •

THE SMALL TOWN WHERE I grew up was a place where being 'different' wasn't celebrated – being different wasn't 'cool'.

I worked hard at fitting in. I worked hard at blending in with the crowd.

Some weren't so fortunate.

Some came to school after doing chores on the farm with the lingering odor of the barn clinging to their ill-fitting clothing.

Some sported hairstyles obviously created under the warm lights of the kitchen by their clipper-wielding mother, siblings waiting patiently for their turn for a trim.

Some sat alone during lunch hour, enjoying sandwiches, wrapped in gently-used wax paper, transported to school in a nondescript black lunch box. The last moments of lunch were spent flattening and folding the paper to take home for tomorrow's sandwich.

Some were just 'different' enough to not belong.

If you didn't fit in, you were subjected to derogatory nicknames. It didn't matter that you were smarter than everyone else. It didn't matter that you could outrun them in a foot race. You were different and that was 'bad'.

I wasn't a bully.

But . . . I didn't stop bullying when I saw it happen. I didn't intervene. I didn't get involved.

Isn't that just as bad as being a bully?

Silence is acceptance.

When you sit back and watch something happen, knowing that it's wrong, knowing that you could make it stop . . . well then, silence is acceptance.

A few years ago I ran into a man with whom I'd attended grade school. He was now a father of two beautiful daughters and had an amazing wife.

He had dared to be a little bit different and he'd paid the price at the hands of our classmates. Ostracized and ridiculed, his school experience had not been pleasant.

I broke down when I saw him and said, "I'm so sorry for not helping you when we were young. I am so sorry that you suffered."

"I forgive you," he said.

I found it difficult to forgive myself.

Silence is acceptance.

Our voice can be our greatest weapon. A collective voice can bring about great change.

Tell Me a Story . . .

• • •

REMEMBER IN THE INTRODUCTION HOW I wished for a three-breasted cousin? Well, if 'three-breasted cousin' was a metaphor for discovering that you have a half-sister then . . . Ta Da!.

A few years ago, I discovered that I had a half-sister.

I know that in the months following the pronouncement I began to slip quietly into a place I knew I didn't want to go to again. That place where my thoughts get twisted and turned and I get angry and sad.

This time I was older and wiser and knew exactly what was happening. I went quickly to my doctor and began taking anti-depressants because I knew that I needed that chemical crutch in order to maintain my footing. I needed to stay sane while the world I knew changed dramatically.

I was very confused. The fact that I had a half-sister was something that would never, ever have entered my mind. My dad could've told me he was a drug addict and I would have been less surprised.

I have another sister? Well.... technically a half-sister, but I don't like to think of her that way because it somehow infers that she is lesser than, and she isn't.

I felt for my mom and I took her lead with the attitude of: If you want me to be mad at Dad then I will be mad at Dad. I kept telling myself that it didn't affect me, that I didn't have the right to be angry or upset.

And I wasn't . . . I was just conflicted. It is like someone took a bulldozer and rammed it into the foundation of a house. Our family foundation was cracked and was threatening to crumble and I didn't know how to deal with that potential reality.

You wonder how your world will be when it stops spinning.

I said that I always wondered what it would be like to have a sprinkling of dysfunction in our family, something to give my writing an 'edge'. I never expected to receive a dump truck of it all at once! The interesting part? I don't write about it. I don't use it as a starting point for any story (other than this one) and I don't lead with it when I do any public speaking.

I think it's because it isn't my story to tell.

My spinning world? Thankfully, once it stopped everyone remained, including a new sister and her children, who I'm happy to call my family. Her name doesn't begin with a "J", but that doesn't make her any less my sister. Love you . . .

Unicorns for Sale

• • •

ONE OF MY VERY FEW (okay, okay, I have *more* than a few) pet peeves in life is being lied to . . . or deliberately misled, or manipulated or bullshitted. I don't think any of us like it. It makes us feel a little dirty, and not in a mud-bath-at-the-spa way. I have a bullshit (B.S.) meter that is very sensitive and reacts quite quickly and accurately around even small, seemingly innocuous piles of manure. Oftentimes, when listening to a conversation, I gauge the B.S. factor of the exchange. A high B.S. factor sometimes results in raucous laughter and snorting coffee out of my nose. That is, until I realize they were serious. Then I get peeved.

I believe that my sensitivity to bullshit came from my upbringing. Yes, I'm going to blame my parents for something else. "Are we almost there?" was responded to with, "Only a few more miles." Hours later (no, not very perceptive at that age), I would realize my parents were lying and that, Hell No! We weren't almost *there* yet.

More from my parents:

"You haven't stopped growing yet, honey. Give it time." (Nope! I peaked early. Please bear in mind that this advice was coming from my five-foot-eight father and five-foot-two mother.)

"Winning isn't everything." (Yes . . . it is.)

"If you cross your eyes, they'll stay that way."

Later in life came, "Do these palazzo pants make me look fat?" and the answer would always be, "No! Of course they don't." But in reality, the wide-legged palazzo pants were not a good fit for a short-legged gal.

Same deal for the tight perm (I looked more like Bob Ross than Diana Ross), the dirndl skirt and my fascination with corduroy vests.

All of these life experiences assisted me in developing my B.S. meter and I feel that now, in my fiftieth year, it's pretty much ninja-level in its accuracy. Basically, I can smell it a mile/kilometer away.

Is honesty the best policy? In business, I 'honestly' believe that it is. Please don't tell me over the phone that the hall will hold two hundred and fifty people when it clearly won't. Don't tell me something will be delivered the next day knowing that it's a logistical impossibility. Please don't over-promise and then under-deliver. Basically . . . please don't intentionally disappoint me. Why? It makes me sad and there's a distinct possibility that a puppy/fairy/unicorn/dolphin might die. Do you *really* want that on your conscience?

So although manure makes for good fertilizer (you should keep it handy for social occasions, with family and friends and hey . . . even blog posts), it won't help a professional relationship grow.

If I had a magic lamp and was provided a wish? Less crap. Oh, and by the way? I've sold out of unicorns . . . Sorry.

The End. Period.

• • •

You know the commercial about dementia where the daughter noticed that her mom, or maybe it was her dad, had bowls and bowls of lemons around the apartment? No? Maybe it was milk and the fridge was full of cartons of milk? Doesn't matter. I can't remember the specifics but the premise was that they had forgotten.

Where am I going with this?

There is nothing that I can do if I develop dementia, but I just realized I currently own three boxes of Triple Pack Tampax in various stages of use. It was like the Three Bears story: One box only had the skinny ones left, the other only the massive green-wrapped tampons remain, and the third box hadn't even been opened yet. It dawned on me that I couldn't remember the last time I needed to utilize these slender, cotton-cloaked Roman fertility candles.

Two months? Three months? Four? Oh.My.Gawd. It has been FOUR months!

I quickly Google 'menopause' and 'period' and the following popped up: "If you are not pregnant, a missed period could indicate the onset of menopause" and "Perimenopause ends when a woman has gone twelve months without having her period."

Shit.

I don't need to be hit on the head to understand that the summer of hot flashes combined with the irregular (or disappearance) of the visit from my period meant that I had joined *that* club. And while we are discussing this, let's discuss the use of the word 'visit' when referring to the arrival of said period. It is not a visit! When I think of a visit I imagine a friend coming over for coffee, not a crazy mood swinging psychopath kicking me in the belly so hard that I am nauseous and bleeding from the Hoo-Ha for an entire week.

Shit. Shit. Shit!

Do you know what bothers me the most?

No, not the excessive facial hair. No, not even the insomnia that will accompany the increasing hot flashes. No, what bothers me the most is that I didn't fully appreciate my last period when I had it. (Also, I could almost qualify as a hoarder having three boxes of Tampax lying around.)

Who knows? *That* period (the one I can't really remember) *could* have been my last period. Ever.

I should have done something special, or documented the occasion in some way. Perhaps a red velvet cupcake to enjoy privately while I lit the remaining boxes on fire?

No, my period, which very well could have been my *last* period came and went without so much as a cramp or a whimper.

What do I do with these boxes now? What is the protocol? Do I display one in a shadow box and throw the rest away? Do I hang onto them until twelve months have passed and only then throw them away? Do I keep them in the bathroom cupboard so that friends might see them and think, "Dayum! Judy still gets her period? What's her secret to youth?"

Do I give them to a friend? Do I advertise them on Kijiji? I can see it now:

FOR SALE: YOUTH & FERTILITY
Serious Inquiries only please. Cash only.

For now, I'm going to do nothing. I'm going to combine the two opened boxes and place them alongside the new, unopened box and wait.

If it is to be . . . it will be.

The End. Period

About the Author

• • •

Judy Kucharuk was born and raised in a rural town in Northern Alberta, Canada. While working part time as a customer-service agent and trainer for an airline company as well as an event planner and producer, she is also a weekly opinion columnist for the *Alaska Highway News* and an on-air columnist for CBC Radio Daybreak North. *Naked Tuesday* is her first book.

Kucharuk has two grown children and currently lives with her husband of over thirty years in Dawson Creek, British Columbia.

For more information, visit her blog at www.judykucharuk.com.

Made in the USA
Charleston, SC
22 August 2016